Praise for
Tee to Green

"Gives the 50+ golfer a road map to success and enjoyment."

—S. Annette Thompson, LPGA Master Teaching
Professional and LPGA T&CP Hall-of-Fame

"Goslin and McGirr tell it like it is. Golf is both a lot harder
and much more fun than it looks! If you are thinking about taking up the game, this is the book for you."

—Becky Morgan, LPGA Tour Professional

"Golf can be intimidating for new players, especially men and
women over 50. The authors' insights and straightforward advice
will help every new player, whatever his or her skill level, to have
fun and feel at home on the course as quickly as possible."

—Pat McGowan, PGA Tour and Champion's Tour
Member since 1978

"Nobody can learn a new skill without lots of quality practice—golf is no exception. Goslin explains why practice is so important for new golfers and offers practical advice on how to make
practice an enjoyable and regular part of your golf experience."

—Dr. Bob Christina, Pinehurst Golf Academy

Tee TO Green

A Guide to Golf After 50

David A. Goslin
with Mary Beth McGirr

Quill
Driver
Books

Sanger, California

Printed in the United States of America.

Published by
Quill Driver Books/Word Dancer Press, Inc.
1254 Commerce Way, Sanger, CA 93657
559-876-2170 / 800-497-4909
QuillDriverBooks.com

Quill Driver Books/Word Dancer Press books may be purchased for educational,
fund-raising, business or promotional use. Please contact Special Markets, Quill
Driver Books/Word Dancer Press, Inc. at the above address or phone numbers.

Quill Driver Books/Word Dancer Press Project Cadre:
Doris Hall, David Marion, Stephen Blake Mettee,
Carlos Olivas
First Printing

ISBN 1-884956-73-4 • 978-1884956-73-7

**To order a copy of this book, please call
1-800-497-4909**

Library of Congress Cataloging-in-Publication Data

Goslin, David A.
  Tee to green : a guide to golf after 50 / by David A. Goslin.
    p. cm.
  ISBN-13: 978-1-884956-73-7 (trade paper back)
  ISBN-10: 1-884956-73-4 (trade paper back)
1. Golf for older people. I. Title.
GV966.5.G57 2007
796.352084'6—dc22

                                                2007036659

Contents

Resources

Foreword

Sharing my love of the game of golf has been a cornerstone of my life for over fifty years. Literally thousands of men and women over 50 have passed through the doors of our Pine Needles Learning Center and/or have attended our women-only GOLFARI® golf schools (recognized as the first golf schools in the country).

I often wonder what people do for recreation later in their lives if they don't play golf. Learning golf in the second half of life is a great opportunity to keep both your mind and body active. Never have I told a student on my lesson tee that he or she was too old to learn golf. In fact, a lot of older novices are attracted to our golf schools, which combine both instruction and camaraderie.

As a youngster growing up in Findlay, Ohio, I loved all sports, but something about golf really grabbed me. When I learned to play as a teenager, I was immediately drawn by the challenge of golf. I soon discovered that golf took dexterity and that timing is far more important than sheer power. Power is nothing without timing. I've always said that it doesn't take a great athlete to be able to play golf. Conversely, great athletes aren't always good golfers. That's part of the beauty of the game.

My golf schools have been special to thousands of older beginning golfers, mainly because of our great instructional staff. Mary Beth McGirr has been one of our Golfari instructors for the past fifteen years. She is knowledgeable, professional, and has a gift for working with older adults who are new to the game. David Goslin is a perfect example of a new "golfer after 50." A busy professional, parent, and avid sportsperson, David didn't pick up a club until age 65. In this unique book, he writes about his experiences learning to play golf, combining good humor and firsthand knowledge of the challenges and rewards golf offers to men and women over 50. Together, David and Mary Beth offer a wealth of information and insights to anyone thinking about taking up this great pastime.

Golf is truly a gift to those who are fortunate enough to discover this wonderful lifetime game. I've been blessed to have it as a part of my life for so many years. I continue to enjoy teaching others to love golf as much as I do... and I know you *can* learn to play golf well after 50 or 60 or 70.

Peggy Kirk Bell
Pine Needles Lodge and Golf Resort

Preface

This book is written for men and women over the age of 50 who are thinking about learning to play golf. Most of these men and women are among the more than 70 million members of the baby boom generation. As a group, this generation is healthier and wealthier than any of the generations that have preceded it. Its members will live longer, spend more money, and take greater advantage of a much larger array of opportunities for personal development and recreation than any previous group of prospective retirees in history. A significant proportion of boomers play a sport or are otherwise physically active, and many consider themselves athletes.

However, only a small fraction of baby boomers are seriously involved in the game of golf. The majority have been preoccupied with work and family responsibilities; some have been discouraged by preconceptions about the game; for example, that it is too time-consuming, or expensive, or not physically challenging, or that it is elitist.

Golf is widely regarded as the retirees' sport. It does require a relatively long time to play, but it is less physically demanding than many other sports. It can be played and enjoyed at all skill levels and has an important social component. Most important, anyone can participate as long as he or she can walk and swing a club. As people approach retirement age, many begin to think about taking up golf. If they have played a few rounds, but never taken the game seriously, they may decide to improve their game. If you fall into one of these categories, this book is for you.

This book describes what it is like to learn to play the game later in life from the perspective of a recent learner, in collaboration with a Ladies Professional Golf Association (LPGA) Master Teaching Professional. A sociologist by training, I spent forty years studying education and the processes by which individuals learn new skills. I took up golf when I retired at age 65. Mary Beth

McGirr has spent her life teaching people of all levels and ages to play golf. Our objective is simple—to help prospective golfers over the age of 50 to:

- Understand and manage the challenges and frustrations of acquiring a new set of physical and mental skills after age 50.
- Set and achieve reasonable goals.
- Gain the knowledge and skills to become at ease on any golf course as quickly as possible.
- Sustain their motivation and enthusiasm for the game.
- Have fun doing it.

Acknowledgments

The person most responsible for the existence of this book is my sister-in-law and collaborator, Mary Beth McGirr. She introduced my wife and me to the game of golf, was my first teacher, and helped me weather many of golf's ups and downs. Most important, her insights into the game of golf provided the inspiration for this project. She exemplifies all of the qualities of a great teacher: expertise, experience, patience, enthusiasm, good humor, and the ability to convey her enjoyment of the game to each of her students.

Several of Mary Beth's professional colleagues, including Barbara Smith, Carol Johnson, and Annette Thompson, reviewed and made valuable contributions to the manuscript.

This book also would not have been written without the encouragement and expert editorial assistance of my wife, Nancy McGirr. Kathy McGirr, another member of the McGirr clan, also provided detailed and constructive comments on an early version of the manuscript. I am deeply grateful to each of them.

Both the book and my enjoyment of the game of golf owe much to my friends and playing partners. George McLennan, Steve Barsony, David Gebara, and Bob Gonzalez deserve special thanks for their substantive contributions to the book and for their good humor, grace, and tolerance of my many erratic performances on the golf course. The many men and women golfers whom I have had the good fortune to meet on the first tee share credit for the ideas and insights contained in the following pages. Errors of commission and omission are solely my responsibility.

Introduction

Myths & Misconceptions
About Golf

Golf is the most fun you can have without taking off your clothes.
—Chi Chi Rodriguez

I swung a golf club for the first time in a college physical education class in 1955. It seemed pretty easy to me at the time, but then I wasn't actually outdoors. We learned to hold a golf club and practiced hitting golf balls into a net inside the college field house. I don't remember how well I did in the class. Apart from a few discouraging experiences on driving ranges, I didn't think much about learning to play golf again until I was ready to retire from my full-time job forty-five years later.

Until that point, career and family responsibilities kept me too busy to seriously contemplate learning golf. I played tennis and squash for exercise and enjoyed both. My perceptions of the game of golf were shaped by conversations with friends and family and by watching Tiger Woods and his fellow professionals play golf on television.

When I relinquished my full-time job, my sister-in-law—a teaching professional—gave me a set of golf clubs and I took up the task of learning to play golf. I approached the task with many preconceptions about both golf and what the learning process would be like. It didn't take me long to discover that many of the things I thought about golf were, at best, only partly true. The following are some of those early preconceptions.

- *Golf takes too much time to play.*

One of the biggest reasons people don't learn to play golf is the perception that it takes too much time to play. Until I retired, the idea of spending five or six hours doing *anything* once or twice a week was simply outside the realm of possibility. To the extent that this describes your perception of golf, some facts support your impressions. Of the 27.3 million adults who report that they play one or more rounds of golf a year, *less than half* play more than eight rounds.

The reality turns out to be more complicated. Playing 18 holes of golf can take a long time, especially on a busy Saturday or Sunday morning. But you don't have to play eighteen holes every time (or *any* time) you go to a golf course. Even on busy weekends, most courses are delighted to take your money to play nine holes, usually at a little more than half the cost of an 18-hole round. During the summer, you can often squeeze in nine holes after work and before cocktails.

There are many things besides playing a round of golf that don't take much time and that you can (and *should*) do to improve your skills. Most courses have practice facilities where you can work on your swing and almost all have putting greens to practice putting (usually for free). Practice can be enjoyable and is good exercise. Moreover, the investment of as little as an hour two or three times a week will pay huge dividends in the speed with which your game improves.

I still spend more time practicing and playing nine holes than I do playing eighteen holes. Moreover, for many retirees, having a sport that takes up a lot of time can be an *advantage,* not a disadvantage.

  • *Golf is not a physically challenging sport.*

Anyone who has watched a golf tournament on television cannot help but be impressed by the skill and mental toughness displayed by tour professionals. But many people still do not think of golf as a serious workout. The pros make swinging a golf club look effortless, they wear long pants and collared shirts, and they don't have to carry their clubs. Except on very hot days, they don't sweat a lot. Recreational golfers don't even have to walk; they can ride around in golf carts with cup holders for their beer or soft drinks. From the outside, golf seems like the antithesis of a good workout, at least as measured by being out of breath and how much perspiration one produces.

Golf is not as strenuous aerobically as running several miles or playing three sets of singles tennis. It didn't take long for me to discover, however, that golf offers formidable challenges, both mental and physical, particularly for anyone 50 or older. Most golf courses are more than four miles long, often stretching across hilly terrain. Playing the game itself requires both flexibility and core-body strength, as well as stamina and the ability to sustain one's mental focus. These are the essential elements of fitness and health for older persons, men and women, alike.

  • *Golf is an exclusive sport.*

Many people who play golf belong to a country club. Golf courses are expensive to build and maintain. The financial viability of many courses depends on a stable group of members who help to defray both the initial investment and the ongoing expenses associated with maintaining and running the facility. In part because of the costs, members of such clubs tend to organize their social and recreational life around their club, its facilities, and its activities. This leads to the perception that golf is not as accessible to those who don't have the money, connections, or desire to join a private club.

Over the last fifteen years, the choices of where to play golf have increased significantly, however. Since 1990, the number of private clubs has remained essentially constant at just over 4,000, while the number of municipal and daily fee courses, including those associated with resorts, has increased from 8,000 in 1990 to more than 11,500 in 2005.

Golf courses where anyone can play encompass an enormous range in quality, cost, and, indeed, overall experience. They include some of the most famous courses in the world, including Pebble Beach and Torrey Pines in California, Pinehurst #2 in North Carolina, and the Black Course at Bethpage on Long Island, NY (all sites of the U.S. Open Championship), along with municipal nine- and eighteen-hole courses in many communities. In anticipation of the arrival of the baby boom generation at retirement age, there has been a dramatic increase in the number of retirement and resort communities built around golf courses over the last several decades. Sixty percent of the nearly 400 courses under construction in 2006 are located in retirement communities.

I play most of my golf at public courses, and the excitement of discovering a new course is as important a part of the game for me as my regular Wednesday morning outing with friends at the local municipal course.

• *Golf is expensive.*

The initiation fee for many of the most exclusive country clubs exceeds $100,000, a set of golf clubs can cost more than $2,000, private lessons are expensive, and it can cost more than $250 to play a round of golf at some famous public courses. It is not surprising that golf has a reputation as being a rich person's sport.

It is true that golf can be an expensive pastime. But it is not necessary to join a country club or pay $250 a round to play on a very good golf course. The median greens fees for 18 holes at public courses in the United States is $34, including a golf cart. It is also not necessary to spend a lot of money on equipment, especially in the beginning. But some lessons are a good idea, a set of golf clubs is necessary, and there aren't many golf courses where one can play for free. A collared shirt is required to play on most courses. In terms of cost, golf is comparable to skiing or scuba diving; it is less expensive than owning a boat or flying an airplane. It is more expensive than going to the movies or playing bridge. But if you calculate the cost of playing golf on an hourly basis, you'll find that most golf courses offer good value.

Men and women over the age of 55 or 60 play at sharply reduced rates on many golf courses, and there are many other ways to reduce costs. My Wednesday morning 9-hole round costs me $8.

- *Golf is a man's game.*

Many more men than women play golf. Of the total number of adult golfers—an estimated 28 million in 2005—nearly 7 million, or 25 percent, are women. Among the 12.5 million "core golfers"—those who play eight or more rounds a year—less than 20 percent are women. More important than the disparity in participation is the fact that historically golf *has* been viewed, by both men and women, as more of a man's game. There are still private clubs where members' wives are prohibited from reserving a tee time on weekends. As most everyone who follows professional golf knows, Augusta National Golf Club, home of the Professional Golfers Association Masters Tournament, still does not admit women to membership. In her book, *The Unplayable Lie: The Untold Story of Women and Discrimination in American Golf*, Marcia Chambers describes how golf has played such an important role in advancing the careers of many influential and not-so-influential men, to the detriment of opportunities for women both in the workplace and on the golf course.

But times are changing, and the situation is changing rapidly. From the growing prestige and visibility of the LPGA Tour, to the elimination of barriers for women's participation at all levels of the sport, to the number of women who are learning to play at all ages, golf is fast becoming easily accessible to women. One's gender is no longer an excuse for not becoming involved in golf. Most important, golf offers many benefits for women.

> • *Golf has many rules and rituals; it is difficult to learn the rules or what to expect on the golf course.*

The game of golf probably has more rules than any other individual competitive sport. This is due largely to the fact that the physical environment—the golf course—plays such an integral part in the game. By design, no two golf courses are the same and every golf course plays differently every time one plays it.

To eliminate subjectivity in counting the number of strokes it takes to complete each hole, the rules of golf literally attempt to take into account *everything* that can happen to a golf ball as it travels almost four miles (on an eighteen-hole course) through terrain that has been designed by both man and nature to make its journey as interesting, if not perilous, as possible. Natural features, including grass that is cut at different heights, trees and fallen tree limbs, leaves, bushes, lakes and streams, bunkers, rocks, hills, and animal holes are all part of the game. Since the overall objective of the game is to take as few strokes as possible on each hole, the definition of what constitutes a stroke and what happens when you encounter obstacles that prevent you from hitting your ball (including when you can't find it.) account for the lion's share of the rules of golf.

I will have much to say about these rules and their implications for recreational golfers later in this book. Suffice it to say here that the overriding goal of golf is to have fun. Unless money or a trophy or bragging rights are at stake, there is no rule that says one has to keep score.

Golf also has many informal rules, traditions, and conventions that may seem mysterious to beginners. These are easily learned and rapidly become part of the pleasures of the game.

> • *Golf is a game in which it is easy to be embarrassed if one is not a very good player.*

Golf typically is played in groups of up to four people. Each player takes his or her turn hitting the ball from the tee at each hole. Thereafter, players alternate hitting their balls, beginning with the player whose ball is farthest from the hole. Inevitably, there is pressure to perform in front of an audience consisting of the other members of your foursome. While this can be intimidating, there is no golfer on the face of the earth who has not topped a ball, or missed it entirely, or hit it into the woods while the other members of his or her foursome stand around watching. Obviously, beginners miss more shots than experienced players. Most novice golfers will be surprised by how tolerant the vast majority of golfers are of mistakes by others in their group.

> • *It is necessary to start at an early age to become proficient at golf.*

It is easier to learn to play almost anything when one is young. At the same time, the game of golf is uniquely structured to make it possible not only for older men and women to learn the game, but to play and compete at a high level of proficiency if they resolve to do so.

There are several reasons for this. Learning to play golf well requires practice. For people who have time to devote to developing the necessary skills, this is a big advantage. Second, different parts of the game require different amounts of the physical capabilities that decline most as we age. Putting, for example, accounts for 40 percent of a golfer's score, yet doesn't require either strength or flexibility, just a lot of practice. Short shots—within fiftyS to 100 yards of the green—also contribute significantly to one's score. Again, the short game depends more upon the amount of practice one is willing to devote to it than on physical strength. Finally, even for those shots that are heavily influenced by the amount of power one can generate (the drive), golf courses give older players an advantage by encouraging them to tee the ball up from the forward (closer to the green) tees.

Despite its challenges, golf is especially accommodating to older men and women. If playing well is an important goal for you, it is certainly achievable for anyone willing to invest sufficient time and effort. If exercise, sociability, and enjoyment of the game itself are more important to you, golf offers the opportunity to participate as often as you wish, without regard to your skill level.

*

Whatever your goals and expectations, this book is aimed at making the experience of learning and playing golf more enjoyable. As a recent beginner, I could not help but be struck by the ups and downs—the frustrations and the exhilaration—associated with the complexity of golf. Discovery is an important part of any adventure, but having some idea about what to expect and how to deal with it will speed up the learning process and make the experience even more rewarding.

How this Book Is Organized

It is not necessary to read this book in any order. In fact, you should look first at sections that "speak to your condition." The following is a brief guide to how the rest of the book is organized.

In Chapter 1, we describe why golf is such a difficult game to play well and what makes it so exciting. The purpose is to give readers a deeper appreciation of both the challenges and the rewards that lie ahead.

Chapter 2 addresses the key physical element in the game of golf: the swing. There is no such thing as a perfect swing, especially when one is starting golf later in life. The goal in this chapter is to provide the foundation on which you can build your own unique golf swing.

Putting the principles on which the golf swing is based to good use is largely a matter of practice, the subject of Chapter 3. It will come as no surprise to anyone who has ever acquired a complex mental or physical skill that such learning depends heavily on practice. The goal is not only to increase the efficiency and effectiveness of your practice time, but also to make practice more fun.

Chapter 4 is about the equipment you need to play golf, including clubs, golf balls, and clothing. Our focus is on the special needs of men and women over 50.

Golf courses can be intimidating places, especially for novices. The goal of Chapter 5 is to help you become at ease on any golf course as quickly as possible. Being relaxed improves your play and that makes golf more fun.

Chapter 6 summarizes the most important rules of the game and the principles that underlie them. We then discuss the conditions under which rules can be, and often are, relaxed.

Chapter 7 introduces the concept of course management. For new golfers over 50, making good choices about shots to try and those to avoid is especially important, as is the capacity to set ego aside when deciding which tees to hit from.

Especially among those who are new to the game, dramatic variations in performance are to be expected, not only from day to day, but from shot to shot. The goal of Chapter 8 is to help you manage golf's ups and downs.

Chapter 9 is for women (and men who play golf with women). Many women approach the game differently from men. This chapter offers encouragement and practical advice about making the most of the many rewards golf has for women.

At the end of each chapter, a section called "Backswings" summarizes the chapter's most important notes.

Finally, the material at the back of the book includes sections on games golfers play, exercises for golfers, resources to help you learn the game, and golf terms you should know.

Chapter 1

Golf Is a Lot Harder (and Much More Exciting) than It Looks

It took me 17 years to get 3,000 hits in baseball. I got that many in one afternoon on the golf course.—Hank Aaron

When I gave up my full-time job, I had two goals. The first was to write a book on motivation and learning in schools. The second was to learn to play golf. Two years later, my book on motivation had been published, but my progress on the golf course had been, to say the least, slower than I expected. Nonetheless, I soon found myself thoroughly addicted to this fascinating game. Golf's frustrations, it turns out, are an important part of what makes the game so rewarding to play. As one of my friends says: "Golf is the game we love to hate."

Having previously spent a bit of time on driving ranges, I had some idea of how difficult it was to hit a golf ball. But I expected that a lifetime of playing a variety of sports would give me an edge when it came to learning the game. How hard could it be to transfer the modest skills developed over more than 50 years of playing tennis, for example, to golf? The answer is: about as hard as playing tennis with golf clubs. Let's look at the reasons why this is so.

After you have learned the rules (which is relatively easy, though there are a lot of them), everything in golf revolves around *building the physical and mental skills necessary to hit a tiny white ball accurately to targets located at various distances away with a variety of clubs under widely varying conditions.*

While golf bears some similarities to other sports that involve hitting a ball, there are several important differences between golf and all the others. It is these differences that make golf so challenging and exciting. They include:

- Golf balls travel a long distance when hit by even average players.
- Golf clubs vary in length and shape.
- Many things affect how difficult it is to hit the ball squarely and what happens to the ball after it is struck.
- The ball is not moving when it is hit.
- Every swing counts.
- Players have time between shots to contemplate these difficulties.

The Thrill of Distance

Of all sports that involve hitting a ball, the collision of a golf club with a golf ball causes the ball to travel the greatest distance, by far. On a good day, the *average* male golfer can hit a drive more than 200 yards (the length of two football fields), or 600 feet. The average woman's drive travels nearly 140 yards. The longest measured home run in major league baseball history is 634 *feet* (not yards), hit by Mickey Mantle in 1960. Professional golfers routinely hit the ball more than 300 yards and longest drive competitions in golf regularly are won by shots that carry over 400 yards, more than *twice* as far as the longest home runs in baseball.

Two factors account for this remarkable contrast between baseball and golf:

- Differences in characteristics of the balls used in the two games, and
- Differences in the clubs used to hit them.

Golf balls are much smaller and lighter than baseballs, and because of their construction, they are much livelier (that is, they bounce farther when struck). Moreover, the dimpled surface of a golf ball is designed to maximize the time the ball spends in the air.

Golf clubs are longer, much lighter in weight, and more flexible than baseball bats, thus permitting higher head speeds at impact in golf even by players like you and me. The combination of clubhead speed and a lighter, smaller, higher compression ball makes it possible for a 50- or 60-year-old novice golfer to, on occasion, hit a golf ball as far or farther than Babe Ruth ever hit a baseball.

The sheer possibility of being able to hit a drive that seems to hang in the air forever, until it is just a tiny dot in the distance, is one of the reasons men and women alike become addicted to the game of golf. Until you have had the experience of watching your ball soar into the sky and waiting, breathlessly, for it to land on the fairway or the green, it is hard to imagine how thrilling it can be to hit a golf ball. The feel and sound of the club hitting the ball cleanly contribute greatly to the sensation.

That's the good news about golf. The bad news is that the farther you are able to hit the ball, the greater the likelihood that your ball will end up some place you don't want it to be, such as in a lake, forest, long grass, or someone's backyard. If the face of your club is only a tiny bit out of alignment with the ball at the moment of impact, your ball can easily travel 20 to 40 yards left or right of where you aimed it. If the path your club takes on the way to the ball is slightly off line, the resulting slice or hook can rob you of a third or more of your potential distance.

Once engaged in the excitement of the game, however, the temptation to "grip it and rip it" becomes almost irresistible. This juxtaposition of high risk and potentially high reward is one of the sources of golf's power to seduce almost anyone.

The Over-50 Advantage

I have played in many foursomes with three other players who could each hit the ball much farther than I can. One advantage older golfers have is that while most of us can't hit the ball as far as many younger players, it is often safer to hit a 150-yard shot than one that travels 250 yards. I can usually count on younger and stronger players hitting several tee shots into the woods while my equally off-line, but much shorter drive remains playable because it doesn't *reach* the trees. As Chi Chi Rodriguez put it, *"the woods are full of long drives."*

Golf Clubs Vary in Length and Shape

Golfers are permitted by the rules to carry up to 14 different clubs in their bags. Golf clubs vary in length and shape according to their purpose, and golfers must learn to:

• Adjust their swings to take account of each club's particular characteristics, and
• Learn how to choose the club that is best suited for each shot they face.

In no other sport that involves hitting a ball is it possible, much less necessary, to change the implement with which one hits the ball from shot to shot.

The Importance of a Good Lie

Except for the first (tee) shot on each hole, most golf shots are not hit under the same conditions. The "teeing ground" (area where golfers are required to hit their first shot on each hole) is mostly level and you are permitted to place the ball on a tee, which reduces (but does not eliminate) the chances you will hit the ground with your club or miss the ball entirely. After your tee shot, however, all bets are off. No matter how good your first shot, the next will be influenced by the ball's *lie*, the spot where it comes to rest on the course. Your ball's lie, in turn, will be determined not only by the accuracy of your first shot, but by the luck of the ball's bounce and roll and the characteristics of the golf course. In no other sport are you as much at the mercy of the gods and the vagaries of the playing field.

In every round of golf you will encounter both "good lies" and "bad lies," no matter how skilled you are. *Every* lie is different, and the ability to hit a ball consistently in such a wide range of situations is the result of practice and experience accumulated over years of playing the game, with more than a little luck thrown in. For the beginner, luck obviously plays a much larger role.

The Ball Isn't Moving when You Hit It

In most sports played with a ball, the ball is moving when you hit it. In golf the ball is at rest. In other sports, players react to the motion of the ball, learned and automatic reflexes taking charge of their muscles as they anticipate the flight of the ball. Ironically and paradoxically, it is easier to hit a ball that is moving than one that is sitting perfectly still.

Every Swing Counts

Many experts have said that the act of hitting a pitch thrown from 60 feet, 6 inches away at speeds of more than 80 MPH with a baseball bat is the single most difficult athletic feat in any sport. To partially compensate for this level of difficulty, baseball players get at least three and often many more swings to put the ball in play. Tennis players have two serves and often several swings to win a point and they don't have to win all of the points, or even all of the games to win their match.

In golf, *every* swing counts, whether you hit the ball well, poorly, or miss it entirely. Moreover, a poorly hit ball often makes the next shot more difficult because of a resulting bad lie. And, the disappointment and frustration that result from a poor shot can generate higher levels of stress, which, in turn, add to the difficulty of the next shot. Thus, mistakes in golf compound in ways not characteristic of most other sports.

Advice from the Pro
"Don't Think of a Pink Elephant"

Have you ever heard the expression: "Don't think of a pink elephant?" What's the first image that pops into your mind? Yes, of course, the image of that huge pink comic animal. The brain only sees the image and doesn't register the "do" or the "don't." This is what happens in golf when we focus on what we don't want to happen. One of the first lessons in golf is always to visualize your ball sailing down that big, wide fairway instead of thinking about avoiding the trees that line the fairway or the pond that lies between you and the green. —Mary Beth

Golf Allows for too Much Thought

All sports make demands on the mind as well as the body. Particularly at high levels of performance, mental focus and concentration are an essential part of every game. In fast-paced games, like tennis or racquetball, however, your reflexes and learned responses take control. In golf there is plenty of time to think about your next shot. And it is up to you to decide when to hit the ball. All this thinking can add significantly to golf's difficulty.

Setting Goals and Lowering Expectations

Recognizing and accepting the challenges inherent in the game of golf is one of the most important steps in learning the game, especially for new golfers over 50. Underestimating its difficulties and setting expectations too high for one's performance in the short term are a prescription for frustration, which takes away some of the fun of the game. Setting realistic goals and understanding what it will take to reach them is key, not only to the learning process, but also to enjoyment of the game itself.

While learning to play golf may be more difficult than you expected, you will quickly discover the following two important things.

- First, it doesn't take long to begin to hit some good shots. The first time you get the ball in the air is exciting. Watching your ball soar down the fairway is a real thrill. Really great shots may be few and far between at first, but that makes them even more rewarding.
- Second, most golfers are not that proficient. Consider the following: In 2005, the average score on an 18-hole regulation golf course was 97. The average score for men was 95. For women the average score was 106. These numbers are for *all adult* golfers, including young players and men and women who have been playing for most of their lives. Only 8 *percent* of all golfers regularly score under 80; only another 20 percent typically score between 80 and 89.

For beginners, it is reassuring to realize that relatively few of the people you play with will be much better than you are.

Advice from the Pro
There Is No "Easy Button"

Many of you may have seen the successful television ad campaign for office supplies expounding the merits of the "Easy Button." One of my older students, frustrated with his game at the time, jokingly asked me where he could purchase an Easy Button. Who could ever put a price tag on such a button—especially when it relates to learning golf? It would be priceless. Unfortunately, there is no easy button when it comes to learning golf. There is no substitute for the P&E factor (practice and experience). When I tell my students that it may take 20,000 or more repetitions to learn a particular skill, I add that it may take 12 months or 12 years. It depends largely on your motivation, personal goals, and the amount of time you are willing to spend. —Mary Beth

Backswings

• It may take longer than you initially expect to see significant improvements in your game. Unless you are an especially gifted athlete, don't expect to break 100 consistently *(or even at all)* for a year or so.

• Your progress will depend largely on the amount of time and energy you are willing to invest in learning and playing. *Both* practice and experience on the course are essential for sustained improvement.

• Lessons from a qualified professional will speed your progress and help to prevent you from developing bad habits.

• Set modest goals for different parts of your game; for example, less than 20 putts in nine holes; half of your drives in the fairway.

• Keep track of your good shots, not your mistakes.

• Don't keep score all of the time. Play games to have fun.

• Try to spend at least a couple of hours a week at a practice facility.

• Work on your physical conditioning, especially strength, stamina, and flexibility.

• Don't feel that you must improve. Play golf for the physical and social benefits.

• Most important, *don't give up.*

Chapter 2

The Swing

Golf tips are like aspirin. One may do you good, but if you swallow the whole bottle, you'll be lucky to survive.—Harvey Pennick

W hen it comes to thinking about the golf swing, golfers can be divided into two main camps. There are those who spend a lot of time analyzing what they are doing (or not doing) and why, and those who don't want to be bothered spending time thinking about their swing at all; they just step up to the ball and whack it. The *analysts* read books on the physics of the golf swing and examine every article in golf magazines that promises an extra fifteen yards on your drive if, for example, you keep your right elbow closer to your side during the swing or end up with your elbows pointing toward the target. The *naturals* assume that with a little coaching and a lot of practice, the feedback they get from seeing where each shot goes and how it feels when they hit a slice or a hook will lead to natural corrections and improvement. Analysts approach every shot with "swing thoughts" to help them remember the correct mechanics. Naturals just try to stay relaxed, focus on the target, and swing away. Analysts try to "make it happen"; naturals just "let it happen."

Who is right? Is there any best way to learn how to swing a golf club? Does it make any difference in the learning process if you are over the age of 50? The answer to all of these questions is probably the same: It depends upon who you are, how your mind works, and what experiences have shaped the way you learn in the past. Some people, including me, think it is helpful to have an understanding of the basic principles underlying any new learning task. Others, including my spouse, find that thinking about the task gets in the way of their learning. Whatever your learning style, *too much information* can be detrimental to anyone's learning.

For the analysts, the following section provides a brief introduction to the mechanics of the golf swing. (The really serious analysts can find much more detail in John Zumerchik's fine book: *Newton on the Tee: A Good Walk Through the Science of Golf.*) Those who prefer not to clutter their minds with such details may want to skip this section.

The Basic Mechanics of the Golf Swing

The mechanics of swinging a golf club are the same as cracking a bullwhip, even though the human body is not as flexible as a whip (if it were, people could probably hit golf balls twice as far as they do). When you crack a whip, the momentum generated by the initial forward motion of the whip handle is progressively transferred to a smaller and smaller portion of the whip as it uncoils until, finally, all of the momentum ends up concentrated in the tip of the whip, which

Advice from the Pro
"Avoid Information Overload"

When you try to learn a new skill by analyzing it, your mind can become filled with so many details and instructions that you become *overloaded* with information. When this "paralysis by over-analysis" occurs, your body becomes incapable of doing what your mind wants it to do. The creative side of your brain can't process all the conflicting messages and intuitively execute the skill. Have you ever observed a child learning to hit a golf ball? Unlike you and me, a child doesn't worry about swinging the "right way." When the child hits a bad shot, the child absorbs the details without analyzing them and instinctively adjusts before the next swing. When you learn through overall awareness of an experience, you learn it at a much deeper level. So be aware of the parts of your body, the motion of the club, and how they work together. As your swing improves, you'll develop the capacity to combine separate bits of information. As a result, you'll find yourself thinking a lot less about different parts of your swing and more about the feeling of the swing as a whole. —Mary Beth

often makes a loud *crack* (as the tip of the whip exceeds the speed of sound).

If you don't happen to have a bullwhip handy, to get the feeling of what happens when you crack a whip, try snapping a towel. Stretch a towel out in a straight line behind you on the floor and hold one corner in your hand. Now swing your arm forward as fast as you can and stop the swing abruptly when your arm passes your body. When your arm and hand stop moving, the towel unwinds in front of you, momentum transferring to a smaller and smaller portion of the towel until it is concentrated at the end, which will be moving much faster than your hand just before it snaps back. Men (mostly) who have experience snapping towels at each other in locker rooms are already familiar with this example.

In a good golf swing, like a whip, two separate levers come into action smoothly and sequentially, ending up with the clubhead traveling at high speed at the point of contact with the ball. The first lever is the rotation of the hips, shoulders, and arms around a vertical axis passing through the spine. The second is the rotation of the club around the hands.

In the backswing, the energy involved in these two separate but coordinated rotations is stored in your body as your shoulders and hips turn as far as they can, then in the arms and hands, which end up above the level of your shoulders. At the top of the backswing, your hips, shoulders, arms, and hands are coiled like a spring, ready to unwind. When you swing, the hips and then the shoulders again turn first, rotating back through their original position, and continuing on until they finish with the hips facing the target. *As the body finishes its turn, momentum is transferred sequentially to the arms, to the hands, and then to the club as they unwind like the whip, with the clubhead striking the ball just as it reaches maximum velocity.* Thus, the following aspects apply:

- Clubhead speed (and therefore how far you can hit the ball) depends upon the coordinated operation of *both* levers, body and hands. Neither, by itself, is sufficient.
- The correct synchronization (timing) of these two actions is key.
- The farther you are able to turn your body (flexibility), the more energy will be stored, and therefore the more power will be generated when the clubhead hits the ball.

Tee Boxes and Colored Markers

Every golf course gives players a choice of teeing off (hitting your first shot at each hole) from any one of three, four or five tee boxes. Each box is delineated by colored markers. Better or stronger players play from tee boxes further back. The scorecard gives the yardage from each tee box to the center of the green for each hole.

The marker colors and what the tee boxes are named vary some from course to course, but the following is somewhat standard:

Black: Professionals
Blue: Experts
White: Men
Gold: Seniors
Red: Ladies

Implications for People over 50

The problem that men and women over the age of 50 encounter in swinging a golf club—*the gradual loss of flexibility*—is exemplified by the fact that, at 17, Michelle Wie could hit a golf ball 300 yards, almost as far as Tiger Woods does. Michelle Wie was not as strong as Tiger Woods, nor was she as experienced. But she was tall and flexible, enabling her to generate enormous leverage and consequently high clubhead speed when she struck the ball.

By age 50, almost everyone, no matter how active physically, has begun to lose some flexibility, as well as strength. For golfers, the decrease in flexibility is at least as important as the loss of strength. As we continue to age, the contortions necessary for a successful swing are more difficult and they place greater strain on the body.

What this means for all of us older folks is:

• We can't expect to hit a golf ball as far as many younger people, no matter how much we practice (or how many weights we lift to maintain our muscles). That's why most golf courses have tee boxes for older and/or less experienced golfers.

• Anything one can do to sustain or increase flexibility is especially useful.

• Maintaining core body strength, particularly the abdominal muscles, is important to reduce the potential for injuries.

• We must be watching for adverse adaptations and adjustments to our swing that arise as compensation for changes in our physical capabilities, particularly loss of flexibility. This is where good instruction can be especially helpful.

The Importance of Instruction

Two truisms in golf are that everyone's swing is different and that anyone can benefit from expert assistance in getting the most out of their capabilities. This is especially true for those who take up the game for the first time after age 50. Developing the proper timing of the several coordinated motions of legs, body, arms, and hands involved in a good golf swing is a complex learning task. Adding to the difficulty is the fact that most people over the age of 50 bring to golf an array of habits formed in other sports that are not helpful to the development of good golf skills.

My experience suggests that it is also more difficult in golf than in many other sports to form a mental picture of what you are doing from how it *feels*. I suspect this is because so many things are happening all at once as you swing a golf club. In this context, an experienced teaching professional performs the same crucial function as the gymnastics coach who helps you to do correct somersaults until your muscles and brain learn what it feels like to do a somersault in mid-air. (Not that any of us over 50 are learning to do airborne somersaults.)

Elements of the Golf Swing

The same basic swing is used to hit with all of the clubs in your golf bag except the putter. Chips and pitches require a shorter swing, but *all shots hit with a full swing* of the club employ the same mechanics and are comprised of the same two elements: the setup and the swing itself. Let's start with the setup. The setup includes *the handhold (or grip), stance, posture, alignment to the target, and position of your body relative to the ball.* Every golf instructor emphasizes the importance of each part of the setup and, although modifications in one or more of these elements may be necessary because of the position of your ball on the golf course (for example, whether it is resting on the side of a hill or under a tree limb that restricts your backswing), consistency ultimately depends upon performing *each element of the setup properly every time.*

The Setup

The Grip

The "hand-hold" or "grip" connects the golfer to his or her club and is fundamental to a good golf swing. The right hand is placed on the club handle below the left (for a right-handed golfer) and it is *vitally important to have a "matching" of the hands.* This means that the palms face each other and the hands work together as a unit.

First, let your arms hang down by your sides. Next, position the handle of the club below the heel pad (by the "lifelines") of the left hand, so that it extends diagonally across the left fingers and palm and upward to the second joint of the index finger. Think of it as laying the club across the "roots" of your left fingers. The fingers then close around the handle of the club. You should feel most pressure in the last three fingers of the left hand.

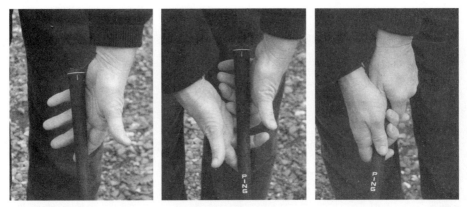

Holding the club.

Next, position the right hand on the club, placing the club more in the fingers of the right hand and cover over the left thumb. The right index finger should be in a slight "trigger" position, creating a gap between the index finger and the last three fingers. The pressure points in the right hand will be the middle and ring fingers. Think of the last three fingers of each hand as the "grippers" and the thumb and index fingers as the "feelers."

There are three common ways to place and/or connect your left and right hands on the club. These methods of holding the club are referred to as *ten-finger* (or baseball), *overlapping* (or Vardon*)*, or the *interlocking* grips. Which method you choose is mostly a matter of personal preference, although finger length, physical structure, and certain limitations, such as arthritis, are factors to consider.

• The *ten-finger* method is self-explanatory. You simply cover your left thumb with the fingers of your right hand and allow all ten fingers to grip the club. It's an easy way to start out before experimenting with the overlapping or interlocking methods. If you have painful arthritis in your fingers, this may be the best grip for you.

• The *overlapping* method is often referred as the Vardon method for Harry Vardon, a great English golfer in the early 1900s. In this popular grip, the right "pinky" finger lies on top of (overlaps) the left forefinger or between the forefinger and middle finger of the left hand. Either place for the overlap is fine; your preference will probably be determined by the size of your hands.

• In the *interlocking* method, the little finger of the right hand is hooked under the forefinger of the left, and it rests between the index and middle fingers. In all three of the handholds the pressure points (last three fingers of the left hand and middle and ring fingers of the right hand) remain the same.

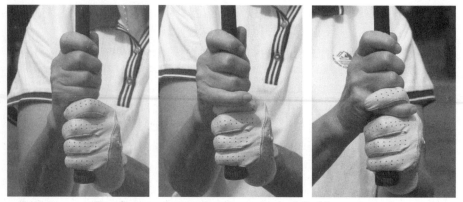

Ten-finger grip, overlapping grip, interlocking grip

Women and men with small hands should try the interlocking grip because it helps to ensure that your hands work together on the club. What's most important, however, is to make sure the grip feels comfortable to you.

Advice from the Pro
Strong vs. Weak Grips

Whatever grip you choose, the "V" formed by the thumb and forefinger of each hand should point just inside your right shoulder. To *strengthen* your grip, rotate both hands slightly to the right, so that the V points to your right shoulder. A stronger grip helps to promote a draw (a shot that curves to the left) and reduces the tendency to slice the ball. Rotation of the hands to the left weakens the grip and promotes a fade (a shot that curves to the right). Most older players should use a strong grip to achieve more distance. —Mary Beth

Advice from the Pro: "Light, Not Tight"

The word "grip" is semantically loaded; it carries a connotation of tightness or extreme pressure. Instead of the John Daly-attributed motto of "Grip It and Rip It," you should be thinking more along the lines of "Hold It and Mold It." It's a completely different idea, isn't it? The term "handhold" is one I like because it defines the concept far more accurately than does the term "grip."

The appropriate amount of pressure on the hands may be described on a scale of 0 to 10, with 10 being the greatest amount of pressure. With a 10 grip, your fingers, hands, arms, shoulders, neck, and even back will feel the pressure. Now, try to exert the least possible amount of pressure on the club. Place your hands on the handle and slide them up and down. This is a 0 on the scale. As you add, hold pressure, find the point where your hands no longer slide down the handle, and then increase the pressure slightly. This is about a 4 on the 10-point scale and generally represents the ideal firmness with which to hold the club. It is strong enough to make sure the club doesn't fly out of your hands on your swing, but not so tight that it increases tension in your arms and shoulders. Think light, not tight. —Mary Beth

Stance

The next aspect to consider is the stance, the position of your feet. When you take your stance, the *insides* of your feet should be approximately shoulder-width apart. A stance that is too narrow makes it harder to keep your balance; too wide a stance negatively affects your ability to turn your shoulders and hips. Your weight normally should be evenly distributed between the feet. (This may vary on occasion, especially for specialty or more advanced shots). It is sometimes beneficial to flare slightly one or both feet. This helps the hips to turn more easily.

Posture

With your feet set, flex your knees and bend forward slightly at the hips, with your weight on the balls of your feet. If you've been a participant in other sports, a good analogy is that of an "athletic position."

You want to achieve a position where your arms hang naturally from your shoulders. Your head stays relatively on plane with the spine or slightly lower. If you have bi-focal or tri-focal lenses in your eyeglasses, sometimes your head must be lowered further to enable you to see the ball out of the top lens.

Stance and posture

Having good posture in golf is important. In the early stages of golf, the posture may not feel natural. Your spine is tilted forward from the hips, as determined by the length of the club, and your head is up and relatively in line with your spine. Try to feel somewhat angular, with easiness in the knees and a tilt forward from the hips.

Alignment to the Target

Golf is truly a target game and it is always important to set up with a target in mind. On the tee, your target may be as long and wide as the entire fairway. As you make progress toward the hole, the target decreases in size. As you approach the green the target may be the depth and width of the green itself. The final target is that 4¼-inch diameter hole.

A visualization that is often used for alignment involves using the image of "railroad tracks." The outside track (farthest away from your feet) is the "target line," which is an imaginary line that runs through the ball and directly to your intended target. The inside track (closest to your feet) is another imaginary line parallel to the target line. It is called "parallel left" because your feet are aligned to the left of the target (for right-handed golfers).

Using an image of railroad tracks for alignment

Ball Position

The fourth element in the setup is the position of your body (stance) relative to the ball. In most cases, the position of the ball between your feet is determined by the length of the club you have chosen to use to hit the ball. With the shorter irons (numbers 6, 7, 8, and 9 and the pitching wedge), the ball normally should be positioned midway between your feet. For longer irons (3, 4, and 5), hybrids, and fairway woods (5-, 7-, 9-, and 11-wood), the ball should be positioned closer to the left foot. With the driver and the 3-wood, it should be positioned opposite the left heel. Your stance should be slightly wider than your shoulders with the long irons and woods.

Ball position with driver; with long irons, hybrids; with short irons

Distance from the Ball

The final component of the setup is the distance of your body from the ball. In your golf posture, with your arms hanging naturally from your shoulders and your hands holding the club properly, the head of the club being used should rest relatively flat on the ground directly behind the ball (this is called *soling* the club). You should not have to bend over farther to reach the ball with your club.

Ready to start the swing

A Perfect Setup, Every Time

As will become apparent in the next section on the swing itself, lots of things can go wrong when you swing the club. You can do much to eliminate mistakes in your swing, however, by making sure that your *setup is perfect every time* you prepare to hit the ball. Your mental checklist should include (1) grip, (2) stance, (3) posture, (4) alignment to the target, (5) position of your stance relative to the ball, and (6) adjustments to any of the foregoing dictated by the ball's lie (for example, whether the ball is lying on the side of a hill). Always try to look at the target from behind the ball before taking your stance, check your alignment by holding your club in line with your feet if you are not absolutely sure about the target alignment, and think about the whether the ball is in the correct position for the club you are using. Establish a pre-shot routine and stick to it *every time.*

The Swing

Literally hundreds of books and thousands of articles have been written on how to swing a golf club. Every issue of every golf magazine contains dozens of tips from experts on how to improve your swing. *There is no substitute, however, for professional instruction when you first take up the game and at regular intervals thereafter to make sure that bad habits have not crept in.* That said, here are brief introductions to each of the major elements of the swing itself.

Like most beginners, I had little meaningful understanding of the basic mechanics of the golf swing when I started. I was taught how to hold a club and where and how to stand relative to the ball. I learned to flex my knees slightly and how far apart to set my feet. I was told to turn my shoulders, keep my left arm extended, and cock my wrists as I began my backswing. Then, thinking about all those professional golfers I had watched on television, I took my club back and swung at the ball. Like most other beginners, the early results were not very encouraging. When I did manage to hit the ball instead of the ground, it usually curved (sliced) sharply to the right. More often than not, the ball simply bounced along the ground.

Advice from the Pro
Match Expectations to Reality in the Beginning

It is important to match your expectations with the reality of how difficult it is to learn a new skill, especially in the beginning. The initial stage of learning involves thinking about your swing, watching, listening, experimenting, and getting feedback about your performance. You are trying to get the general concept of the swing. Numerous gross errors and very erratic shots characterize this early stage. You should expect nothing more than a combination of topped shots, whiffs, wild directional blunders, with a few (very few) great shots thrown in to keep you from becoming too discouraged. —Mary Beth

Since the beginning of my golf endeavors, my swing has improved, though not as quickly as I had expected or hoped. In reflecting on my experience, the following six ideas stand out as essential to the basic golf swing:

- *Rotation.* The single most important component of

the golf swing (more important, even, than actually swinging the club) is the weight transfer produced by the rotation of the body around its vertical axis, beginning initially with the shoulders and then followed sequentially by the hips and legs. The transfer of weight is fundamental both to the ultimate development of clubhead speed (power) and consistency in the path of the club to and through the ball. You can practice this element *without a golf club* by crossing your arms over your chest or by putting your hands on your hips, spreading your feet apart as you would before you swing a club, and turning your upper body so that it faces 90 degrees (or more) to the right (assuming you are right-handed).

As you rotate, you will feel increased tension in your abdominal muscles and on the inside of your right leg. The farther you turn, the more your left heel will want to lift off of the ground. After you have turned as far as you can go to the right, rotate back *through your starting position*, starting with your hips and pushing off of your right toe until your shoulders and hips are facing ninety degrees to the left (toward your imaginary target). Now your right heel will be completely off the ground.

Address, backswing, follow-through, finish

Tip for Golfers over 50

Allow your left heel to lift off the ground in your initial turn to the right. This will make it possible for you to increase the radius of your turn, thereby compensating, in part, for a relative lack of flexibility. Most professionals keep their left foot and heel firmly planted in order to increase torque and therefore power, but they are younger and more flexible than we are.

Practice Tip

You can practice your rotation anywhere and anytime you find yourself standing still; for example, in line at the supermarket or waiting for an elevator. Keep track of how many people ask you: "Practicing your golf swing?"

• *Left arm extended.* The second lever involves cocking your wrists during the backswing. The wrist cock depends upon *keeping your left arm extended* as you take the club back in preparation for your swing. One way to get the feel for this motion, and the associated wrist cock, is to push out and to the right with the heel of your left hand as you turn your body and swing the club up and backward. At the top of your backswing, your left arm and the club should form a right angle. Your thumbs should be pointing upward.

Tip for Golfers over 50

Shorten your backswing. Most beginners (indeed, many golfers) take the club too far back in the belief that a huge wind-up will create more power. Proper coordination of the rotation of body, and of the arms and hands, is much more important than the length of the swing. The bigger the backswing, the harder it is to get the timing right and to keep the swing on the proper plane through the ball on the downswing (i.e., to hit the ball cleanly).

Practice Tip

Practice your backswing in front of a mirror. Make sure your left arm is extended all the way to the top. You will be surprised by how far upward and how far backward the clubhead travels. If the clubhead drops down so that the club points at the ground behind your head, your backswing is too long.

• *Tempo.* The third major component of the swing is the proper sequencing of the operation of our two levers in the swing itself. After the backswing, the body *must* start its rotation back toward the ball a fraction of a second *before* the arms and hands start the downswing. The rotation of the body back toward the ball is initiated by pulling back on the left hip and pushing off on the inside of the right foot—hips preceding shoulders and then arms as the body unwinds like a spring. For me, this was the most difficult element of the swing to learn, and still it is the hardest to accomplish consistently on the course. Especially when one is faced with a difficult shot, or tries to hit the ball especially hard (perhaps to get it over a hazard), it is nearly impossible to resist the tendency to start the arms and hands before the body. The result is almost always disastrous, usually with the club hitting the ground before it strikes the ball. This is called "chunking."

Advice from the Pro
Try Humming a Tune

Some golfers find that humming the right tune helps them find the pause in the transition from backswing to downswing. "Hell—oooooo (backswing), Dolly (downswing)" works for some people for a full swing.

The "Blue Danube Waltz"—"Da, da, *da*, da ...(backswing)...D*a*." works for a relaxed ¾-swing (used in pitching). —Mary Beth

• *Inside-Out Path.* The path of the clubhead from the top of your backswing to the point where it strikes the ball influences not only the direction the ball takes as it leaves the tee, but also its spin. Because of the ball's aerodynamic design, the direction of its spin has a powerful effect on its flight. If the ball is spinning in a clockwise direction (around a vertical axis) the ball will turn right (a fade, or slice). If it is spinning in a counterclockwise direction, it will turn left (a draw, or hook). An inside-out path helps to ensure that the clubhead is squaring to the ball when it strikes it, thus imparting the proper (counterclockwise) spin and preventing the dreaded slice, the bane of most beginners' experience.

Stay on the Inside-Out Path

If you have turned your upper body properly, your hands will be slightly inside (on your side of) the ball at the top of your backswing. When you swing downward on a direct path to the ball from this position, it is likely to feel as though you are hitting the ball out to the right. The mind's urge to compensate for this feeling by pulling the club to the left is almost overwhelming. To keep your swing on an inside-out path, it helps to focus on keeping your right elbow close to your body on the down-swing. A swing thought that may be helpful is: *Swing to the hip pocket.*

• *Maintain the power L.* The next to the last step in hitting the ball with maximum power is to maintain what Mary Beth calls "the power L." As noted above, the power L is the 90-degree angle formed by your extended left arm and the handle of the club after you have cocked your wrists at the top of your backswing. It is the second of the levers in our whip, and maintaining this angle as long as possible is key to increasing clubhead speed through the ball.

The power L

Advice from the Pro
Where Is the "Whoosh?"

To get a feeling for what it's like to accelerate the club through the ball, turn one of your clubs upside down and hold it close to its head. Now, try swinging it. If you are maintaining the power L properly, you won't hear the "whooshing" sound of the club handle passing through the air until the bottom of your swing. —Mary Beth

• *Follow-through.* The last important element of the basic golf swing is the follow-through. Sustaining the momentum of the clubhead through impact with the ball depends upon letting your arms, hands, and the club continue to swing freely after impact as far as they can go. The swing ends with your belt buckle facing the target, your elbows up in front of you, and the club above your head. This is the point where you pose for a picture demonstrating your perfect golf swing (whether you have hit the ball or not).

Advice from the Pro
Video Analysis Can Be Very Helpful

People differ in the extent to which they rely on sound, feel, or visual information in the learning process. For visually oriented learners, video analysis of their golf swing can be especially useful. Video also allows teachers to see details of the swing that the human eye cannot capture. —Mary Beth

Advice You'll Get: "Keep Your Head Down."

As a new golfer, I am willing to wager that the most frequent piece of advice you'll get from other golfers when you're on the course is "remember to keep your head down." This unsolicited tip usually comes when you've just topped a ball (hit the top of your ball with your club, causing the ball to bounce along the ground). The underlying assumption is that lifting your head, perhaps to watch the flight of the ball, caused the error. It sounds logical.

Like many adages, there is some truth to this advice about the golf swing. It is certainly true that standing up straight in the midst of your swing can make it difficult to hit the ball solidly. But your head usually is *not* the problem. Poor posture, lack of rotation, and a faulty weight transfer are more likely at fault. More important, keeping your head down through the swing and follow-through robs you of the power and consistency that come from swinging the club on a plane, with proper rotation and good balance. Bottom line: Focus on your rotation, balance, and the inside-out path of the club and forget about merely keeping your head down.

Overcoming Lifelong Mindsets

Much of what happens in golf contradicts many lifelong assumptions about how the world works that have stood you in good stead over the years and are ingrained in your mind and muscles. Examples of golf's contradictions to lifelong mindsets include the following:

- *Down goes up.* Hitting down and through the ball makes it go up in the air because of the angle of the club face. Trying to scoop the ball up almost always results in the bottom of the club hitting the top of the ball, with the result that the ball bounces along the ground instead of flying up into the air.
- *Left goes right and right goes left.* Aiming left usually causes the ball to go to the right, because of the clockwise spin your swing puts on the ball (a fade, or slice). Conversely, aiming right most often causes the ball to turn left (a draw, or hook).
- *Swinging harder leads to longer shots.* A smoother, more relaxed swing almost always results in better contact and a longer shot than attempting to hit the ball extra hard. Unless you are Tiger Woods, swinging harder more often than not causes you to tighten up, throwing off the timing and mechanics of the swing. The result is poor contact and/or slower clubhead speed. Mary Beth tells her students: "Swing smoothly and just put up with the extra distance."

Swing Thoughts

You have completed your perfect setup and are ready to take your shot. What thoughts should be going through your mind as you prepare to start your backswing? The literature of golf is full of advice about "swing thoughts." If there is any single theme that emerges from the millions of words written about swing thoughts, it is that trying to keep too many (usually more than one or two) thoughts in your mind is more harmful that helpful.

Advice from the Pro
Limit Your Swing Thoughts

It is critical that you learn to condense and simplify your swing thoughts. It's simply not possible to play good golf with a lot of mechanical swing thoughts cluttering your mind. When good golfers are asked about their swing thoughts, it's invariable that the better they are playing the less likely they are to be thinking about mechanics and specific swing thoughts. In fact, imagine for a moment those few "perfect" shots that you've been able to create. What were you thinking? Probably nothing. How did it feel? Effortless is the adjective I hear most frequently.
—Mary Beth

As Your Swing Improves

With instruction and practice, you will hit the ball with more consistency and power with each of your clubs. You will also begin to get a feel for the things that cause the ball to travel in a straight line or curve left or right. As you accumulate experience on the golf course, you will also learn how to adjust your stance and swing to take into account conditions in which you find your ball. Experience on the course, plus greater control over the flight of the ball, make possible more creativity in the shots that you are able to both *imagine and make.* This adds greatly to the enjoyment of the game.

Draws and Fades

When the ball turns gently to the left (for right-handed golfers), it is called a *draw.* A sharp left turn is a *hook.* Both are caused when your swing imparts a counterclockwise spin to the ball. Hooks are not good, almost always ending up shorter than desired and often in the trees or out-of-bounds. In contrast, draws travel farther than any other shot because their spin causes them to bounce and roll forward when they land. A draw is produced by an inside-out swing path with the club face slightly closed at impact. Strengthening your grip, closing the face of the club slightly at address, and closing your stance (turning your feet a little to your right at setup) can help you learn to draw the ball. You should practice these adjustments to your swing on the range before trying them on the golf course. You will probably find that it is easier to hit a draw with your irons than with your metal woods or driver in the beginning.

A *fade, or cut,* is the opposite of a draw. The ball turns gently right (for a right- handed golfer). If it turns sharply right, it's a *slice,* the most common mistake made by beginners. Fades and slices are caused by a clockwise spin of the ball. Fades do not travel as far as draws, but are often used by expert golfers (who usually don't need extra distance) for increased control. A fade is produced by: 1) weakening your grip, 2) maintaining your wrist cock longer in your downswing, and 3) opening the club face slightly. If your clubhead is traveling on an outside-in path, you are more likely to hit a slice than a fade.

Advice from the Pro
The Ideal Swing Doesn't Exist

There is no such thing as the perfect swing. Even among professionals, there is considerable variation, although professional swings may all look similar to the untrained eye. Everyone develops their own particular style and as you spend time on the golf course you will encounter examples of quite different swings, many of which work reasonably well for their owners. Moreover, as we age, we adapt our swings to accommodate changes in our bodies, not to mention our minds.

There is not a swing for everyone, but everyone has one swing. —Mary Beth

Backswings

- Stretch to maintain flexibility.
- Exercise to build core body strength.
- Pay attention to the fundamentals of grip, stance, alignment, and ball position.
- Establish a routine to ensure a perfect setup, every time.
- Use all your leverage: rotation, rotation, rotation.
- Timing is everything; think pause at the top of your backswing, or hum a tune to find the right tempo.
- Practice whenever and wherever you can: at home in front of a mirror, waiting for elevators, at the bank, and in the supermarket checkout line.

Chapter 3

Practice, Practice, Practice

*"There are no born golfers. Some have more natural ability than others, but they've all been made. —*Ben Hogan

A few months after I retired, my coauthor, Mary Beth McGirr, took my wife and me out onto a golf course for the first time. We had taken a few golf lessons and spent some time on a practice range, but neither my wife nor I had ever actually tried to play the game on a real golf course. Fortunately, there were few people around. Mary Beth, like all good teachers, was patient with us. I can recall vividly how effortlessly she hit ball after ball exactly where she intended it to go. When I did manage to hit the ball, it usually bounced along the ground for twenty or thirty yards. Sometimes, the ball went in the direction I had aimed it, often it did not. Only occasionally was I successful in getting the ball into the air. The harder I tried, the worse it got. After an hour or so of my growing frustration, Mary Beth turned to me and said: "Don't worry, it takes at least 20,000 repetitions to achieve consistency."

Learning *any* skill requires practice. No matter how innately talented you are, complex mental or motor skills don't materialize overnight. This is true whether you are learning to speak a foreign language, play a musical instrument, or hit a golf ball. Plenty of students have gone to bed with a textbook under the pillow, hoping that they will awake knowing how to speak a foreign language or do enough math to pass tomorrow's test. Alas, this never works.

Advice from the Pro
Do You Play the Piano?

One of my older students is a concert pianist. She was getting quite frustrated with her swing and lack of directional control. I asked her how many hours she spent practicing before a big concert. Her response was up to *six hours* of practice *per day*. The analogy put golf into perspective for her because she rarely practiced more than an hour *per week* for golf.

Professional golfers are like the concert pianists in their field. Countless hours have been spent hitting practice balls and working on the short game. When I was coaching college golf at Wake Forest University, Billy Andrade was in college. On one particular afternoon, I teed off with the girls on my team while Billy was on the green practicing his putting. Two hours later when we approached the 9th green, there was Billy, still practicing his putting. He went on to become a successful PGA Tour professional, but the memory of seeing him practice putting for hours still stands out in my mind. —Mary Beth

Practice is particularly important for those who take up golf later in life. Most people are accustomed to doing whatever physical activities they do reasonably well. If you play a sport—for example, tennis or racquetball—the chances are that you are comfortable with the level of your game, you are at home on the court, and you are used to playing with others who play at your level. Playing once or twice a week enables you to maintain your skills even though you may not be as strong or as fast as you once were. Your experience playing the game helps to compensate for the slow decline in physical capabilities and you actually may be playing better than at any time in your life.

Learning an entirely new sport is a major undertaking. It is particularly stressful when you find yourself playing with (and in front of) people who have been playing the game for years. If you think of yourself as a reasonably good athlete, you both *want* and *expect* to reach a minimal level of competence quickly. *Unlike other sports, however, most people can't improve their golf skills simply by playing the game.* This is why practice is more important in learning to play golf than in almost any other sport.

The Importance of Repetitions

When you are trying to learn a motor skill, practice involves repeating the appropriate muscle movements until they become ingrained in "muscle memory." Although there are big differences among people in how many repetitions it takes before the necessary memories are stored in their muscles, there is no doubt that the more complex the skill, the more "reps" it takes to learn it. Thus, for most people, it is likely to take thousands of repetitions to develop a consistent and predictable golf swing.

What may come as a surprise is the realization that it is almost impossible to get the repetitions necessary to develop a consistent swing merely by playing golf. Let's do the math. In an eighteen-hole round of golf, even a beginner is unlikely to take more than sixty full swings at the ball (the pros take around thirty), not counting practice swings or chips and putts (which involve separate skills and account for almost half of a typical golfer's total score). Thus, it takes several eighteen-hole rounds of golf—each taking four or five hours—for a golfer to accumulate a few hundred repetitions of the swing. By contrast, in any good singles match in tennis you will easily hit the ball several hundred times. It is entirely possible to improve your tennis game in a relatively short period of time simply by playing tennis. *However, unless you are unusually talented, it is unlikely that your golf game will improve without practice, no matter how many rounds of golf you play.*

So, how does one get the thousands of repetitions it takes to learn to hit a golf ball with consistency? The answer is to find a place where you can swing a golf club at a ball without endangering others or damaging property (a serious matter, considering how far a golf ball travels when hit). Most full-size golf courses have practice facilities that include a driving range where you can practice hitting balls with each of your clubs, putting greens, and often areas where you can practice chipping, pitching, and bunker play. Unless the golf course is part of a private club, anyone can purchase a bucket or bag of range balls and make use of the facilities, whether they play golf on the course or not. In addition, there are dedicated commercial driving ranges in most areas where you can go to hit balls. If you can't get to a practice facility, there are things you can do at home or in any modest size open space to improve your swing. Finally, there are ways to increase the number of repetitions you get while playing on many golf courses, which will be discussed later in this chapter.

Advice from the Pro
Practice Makes Permanent

There's an old saying that *practice makes perfect*, but the reality is that *practice makes permanent*. Any skill that you practice repeatedly, whether it is performed efficiently or not, becomes a habit. It absolutely makes no sense to me when I see people toiling away on the practice tee—practicing and grooving bad habits. Therefore, always strive for *perfect practice* so that you can groove good swing skills. For example, holding the finish of your swing until the ball stops rolling helps your muscles remember a balanced finish. The importance of practicing mechanically correct skills cannot be overstated. —Mary Beth

The purpose of this chapter is to help you find ways to practice the skills that you will need to play a respectable round of golf and to get the most out of the time you do spend practicing. The goal is to make your practice both efficient and enjoyable. Let's begin by reviewing the skills you need to play golf.

Essential Skills of the Game of Golf

Four major skill sets are integral to the game of golf. It is possible to work on all of them without actually playing a round of golf.

- *The full swing.* The basic swing is used to hit the ball varying distances with all of the clubs in your bag, except the putter. The stronger and more flexible you are, the farther you can hit the ball with each of your clubs. Accuracy is the name of the game, however, and attaining accuracy takes lots of practice.
- *Pitching and chipping.* These shots involve shorter swings and are used to hit the ball for shorter distances. In general, a pitch is used to loft the ball over an obstacle, such as a bunker, and minimize the distance it rolls after it lands. A chip has a lower trajectory and rolls farther after it lands. Most golfers carry at least one highly lofted club designed for pitching the ball. Any club, except the putter, can be used to chip. Learning to hit really good chips and pitches helps

to compensate for the over-50 golfer's disadvantages in strength and flexibility.

- *Bunker play.* Hitting the ball out of the sand in bunkers is a special skill that requires its own practice. Not all practice facilities have bunkers for practicing these skills, but there is no other way to work on these skills.

- *Putting.* This is the stroke used to roll the ball into the hole on the green. This skill is the older golfer's most powerful weapon and the one that is easiest to practice.

Caution for New Golfers over 50: Don't Overdo It

Before looking at each of these options, a word of caution, especially for older people: *Don't overdo it.* Now that I've convinced you that it will take thousands of repetitions in order to hit a golf ball with consistency, some of you may be tempted to see how quickly you can hit ten or twenty thousand balls, thereby achieving your goals more quickly. There are two important reasons why this is a bad idea. First, you could injure yourself. Hitting a golf ball requires using a lot of different muscles in ways that you may or may not have used them in the past. It also requires both flexibility and muscles that are essential to protect critical joints (knees, shoulders, elbows, hips) and other parts of the body, including, especially, the back, from injury. It takes time to build strength, particularly as one gets older. If you are over 50, the odds are that you aren't either as strong or as flexible as you were when you were 30, or even 40. Thus, it makes sense to have a program designed to gradually build strength, flexibility, stamina, and skills at the same time.

Second, there is a lot of scientific evidence that *spaced trials* are more effective in promoting high-quality learning than *massed trials*. Both brain and muscles can only absorb so much new information at one time;

at some point, additional repetitions are wasted. Worse, as muscles tire, it becomes more difficult to repeat the high-quality swing that you have been working on, with the result that it is easy to learn bad habits. Bottom line: it is much more effective, and safer, to hit 50 or 100 balls at the practice range on three different days than it is to hit 300 balls all at once.

Practicing the Full Swing

The following are six ways to practice your full golf swing away from the golf course, each of which has its advantages and disadvantages:

• *Hitting real golf balls on a practice range.* This is the closest thing to playing golf (although it isn't perfect), and this is where most people spend most of their time practicing. Most practice facilities charge between $4 and $6 for a bag or bucket of forty-five to fifty balls. All public and many semiprivate golf courses with practice facilities, including resorts, will let you use their range whether you play golf or not. Many golfers also try to allow time to warm up on the practice range before they play a round.

• *Hitting real golf balls in a simulator.* An in-creasing number of golf learning centers, practice facilities, and even stores that sell golf equipment are installing simulators that enable you to hit real golf balls into a wall-sized mat on which is projected the image of a golf course. Sensors feed information to a computer that shows the flight of the ball when you hit it, along with detailed feedback on launch angle, ball speed, distance, and the like. Practice in a simulator feels like the real thing, it provides much more information than you get on the driving range, and it's especially great on a rainy or snowy day. You can even play a round of golf on a famous course. Our local sporting goods store charges $12.50 for a half hour in the simulator.

• *Hitting real golf balls into a net.* A net is a poor substitute for a full-size range because it restricts the flight of the ball and therefore prevents you from getting full feedback on the results of your swing. But a net is better than nothing when you can't get to a regular practice facility or when weather conditions prevent you from being outside.

• *Hitting plastic golf balls in more restricted spaces, such as your backyard.* Plastic balls will fly only 40 or 50 yards no matter how hard you hit them, but they are designed to mimic the flight of a real ball. Thus, the flight of the ball will tell you when you slice, hook, or hit the ball straight. Most important, you won't break any windows with plastic balls. The disadvantage is that you don't get the feel of hitting a real golf ball.

• *Clipping tees.* You can work on your swing any place you can put a tee in the ground and swing a club by practicing clipping the top of the tee. Obviously, try to choose a place where your club doesn't do too much damage when you hit the ground in front of or behind the tee.

• *Indoor swing exercises with or without a club.* When it's cold or wet (or dark) outside, you can practice your swing in front of a mirror using a short club designed to feel like a full-sized club, but which won't damage furniture or the ceiling. Even without a club, you can practice your swing movements and rhythm almost anywhere.

Getting the Most Out of Range Practice

The first challenge is to find a practice facility that includes at least a driving range, and, if possible, areas to practice bunker play, chipping, and pitching. Convenience should be a primary consideration, since the closer it is to your home or office, the more likely you are to use it. If you are retired or have a more flexible schedule, so much the better. Like golf courses, practice facilities are always less crowded on a weekday than on weekends.

If you have a choice, look for a range where you are able to hit balls off grass instead of artificial mats, which are more durable but less realistic (even the best facilities are likely to switch to artificial mats in the winter). Most practice facilities will have a putting green. A really good facility will also have areas for practicing bunker shots (out of the sand) and chips onto the green. Some will have complete practice holes, where you can hit multiple balls to a green.

Advice from the Pro
Establish a Practice Routine

You've bought a couple of bags/buckets of practice balls and have found a spot on the practice range. What happens next? How do you organize your practice session to make the most of it? Begin with several minutes of stretching exercises to loosen up your muscles, followed by a dozen or so practice swings with two clubs together or use a specially designed weighted practice club.

It is helpful to establish a practice routine like the one I recommend my students follow. It's based on the 20-20-20 rule. For example, if you have one hour to practice, then spend twenty minutes practicing your short game, twenty minutes on the full swing, and twenty minutes on putting. This allots two-thirds of every practice session to your short game (the quickest and easiest way to lower your scores).

- Start with a short iron and warm up for ten minutes with short and long chips (all one-lever swings and less than waist-high backswings). Then progress to ten minutes of pitching. Use a variety of targets to practice distance control (golf towels laid out at various distances work great).

• To practice your full swing, hit five to ten balls with each of the odd or even numbered irons in your bag (PW-8-6 or 9-7-5). Go through the routine that you use on the course and hit to a specific target. Progress to your fairway woods and/or hybrids and then use your driving club (either a driver or 3-wood). Be sure to pick out a larger target (i.e. between two flags) to simulate an imaginary fairway. If you have a few minutes left over, alternate the types of shots (as if to simulate the shots you would need to use on any real given hole).

• Move to the putting green and spend twenty minutes practicing your putting mechanics as well as your feel and speed. Practice your technique by making ten putts from two feet, three feet and four feet. You'll be amazed how practicing *making* putts will help your confidence on the course. Also, practice your distance control. A good drill for this is to putt from the center of the practice green to the edge, trying get each ball as close to the edge of the green as possible. Another is to putt nine holes using one ball (just like on the course). Your goal is to average a maximum of two putts per hole.

—Mary Beth

Games to Play while Practicing

As important as range practice is, it is important to keep in mind that the practice facility is not the golf course. It is one thing to hit ten good shots in a row on the driving range; it is quite another to hit one good shot on the course. There are games you can and should play to make the transition from the practice range to the course easier. The simplest is to play a round of golf on the range. After you have warmed up, pretend that you are starting with your drive on the first hole of a regular course. After your tee shot, hit a combination of your fairway woods and irons to targets at different distances. Then, start over with another "tee shot," followed by using your woods and irons as appropriate. You can make this exercise as realistic as you want; the important thing is to practice shifting from one club to another, and from one distance to another, as you would do in an actual round of golf.

Chipping and Pitching Practice

Some practice facilities also have places where you can practice your short game, including pitching and chipping. But it may not be necessary for you go to a practice facility to practice these shots. As soon as you start playing golf, you will begin to accumulate used golf balls, some that you have played with, others that you find on the course, and others that friends donate (whether you want them or not) when they hear you have taken up the game.

With a basket of balls, a small mat to hit from (so that you don't rip up your lawn), and a plastic tube designed to pick up balls you can practice hitting chips and short pitches in any twenty-five-yard to forty-yard open space where you won't endanger other people, pets, or windows if a shot goes astray.

Just as with the full swing, it is important to practice hitting consecutive shots to targets at various distances, as will be necessary on the golf course. Outside of a practice facility, however, it is more difficult to find a place where you can practice hitting balls out of different lies in real grass (or dirt, or a combination thereof) without doing real damage to your yard or the local park.

Advice from the Pro
Play "Up and Down"

If you can find a practice green with no one practicing on it, play a game of Up and Down by yourself or with a friend. Take half a dozen balls and play each of them from off the green to a different hole. Try to get each ball up (onto the green) and down (into the hole) in as few strokes as possible. Set a personal par at three or four per ball and see whether you can do better than a score of eightenn to twenty-four for six balls. —Mary Beth

Bunker Play Practice

For me, learning to hit shots out of the sand traps, more properly known as "bunkers," has been a major challenge. Part of the problem is that not every practice facility has bunkers where you can practice, and this is one skill you can't work on easily in your backyard. To add to the difficulty, the texture of the sand varies greatly from one bunker, and one course, to another, and every lie is different. Building confidence in one's ability to hit the ball consistently out of the sand takes practice and experience on different courses. This is one of the skills you should work on during your practice rounds by yourself or with a friend. In the meantime, of course, you can try to avoid hitting your ball into bunkers in the first place.

Pot bunker at the PGA Learning Center

Putting Practice

For everyone over the age of 50, the most important statistic to remember when you are learning to play golf is that 40 percent of your score in a typical round of golf is made up of putts. Putting doesn't take much strength or even coordination. However, it does take a lot of practice, which you can do at most golf courses and even in your living room for free. Putting, therefore, is the over-50 golfer's secret weapon because you can become just as good—or better—at putting as players half your age.

Nearly all golf courses, whether or not they have a driving range or other practice facilities, *have a putting green* for practicing putts. Any course that is open to the public will let you practice putting to your heart's content, whether you play a round of golf or not. At our local municipal course, there are always men and women on the putting green, many of them golfers who practice for hours without setting foot on the course itself.

There are three separate, but related, skills that must be mastered to putt well:

- *Distance control.* Learning to hit the ball just hard enough to get the ball close to the hole. This is called *lagging* your putt.
- *Accuracy.* Learning to hit the ball in the direction you want it to go.
- *Reading the green.* Learning to judge whether the ball will roll up hill or down, and whether it will break right or left, or roll straight. Your judgments about the slope of the green determines how hard you should stroke the ball and where you aim it.

Just as with practice on the driving range, it is helpful to use one or more routines to organize your time on the putting green. Golf instruction books and magazines are packed with different drills to help you improve your putting. One simple routine is to start by putting two balls into the hole from two feet away, then from four feet, then six feet. Each time you miss, you must start over from two feet. In order to reach six feet, therefore, you will have to sink six putts in a row. Another is to play a mini-game as described in the box below.

Advice from the Pro
Play a Mini-Game to Practice
Playing the Game

I like to start players thinking about playing before they even step onto the golf course for the first time. For example, start with nine holes of putting. Select a sequence of cups of varying distances on the putting green and, using one ball, putt these holes in the same sequence three times. Don't keep score the first time; just get a feel for the varying distances and become aware of the breaks (slope) of the putting surface.

Putt the same nine holes in the same order a second time and keep track of how many times your score is three putts or less per hole. From then on, keep track of your score as if every hole was a par 2 (for example, if your first four scores were 3,4,1,2, you'd be two over par after four holes).

Remember that a good putting stroke does not require much physical strength, but it does require a tremendous amount of practice and experience. This drill of using one ball and putting a different distance each time simulates what happens on the real golf course and gets you accustomed to keeping score.
—Mary Beth

Practicing Using these Skills on the Golf Course

It is one thing to learn the foregoing skills at the practice facility or in your backyard. It is another to apply them under the

Older Golfers: Don't Forget to Straighten Up.

World Golf Teachers Hall of Fame member Peggy Kirk Bell has a word of caution about putting practice: "It can be hard on your back. I always straighten up between every putt and pause briefly. It's too much stress on your back to stay crouched over in your putting stance for too long."

widely varying conditions found on the golf course. Of course, the more you play golf, the more quickly your game will improve. But it is possible to practice your shots on almost any course at some times of the day, or week, or year. Very few golf courses are crowded all of the time, year round. On weekdays in the afternoon or early evenings, when it's too cold or hot, and in the off-season (if there is one), many courses are not crowded. Any course will be happy to take your money for nine or 18 holes and, even though it is usually against the rules, no one will notice if you play more than one ball on each hole, re-hit shots that you miss, practice hitting several chips from off the green on some holes, or repeat your putts. *You must make sure, however, that you never delay other golfers with your practice; be alert and step aside to let any other groups or individuals play through.*

It is much better to walk when you are playing a "practice round," and a pull or push cart that allows you to roll your clubs instead of lugging them on your back is an absolute must for us older guys and gals (see Chapter 4). There is no reason you can't play a practice round with a friend, but I find that I can try many more shots and get much more practice in less time when I play alone.

Combining Practice on the Range and a Course

When I took up golf, one of the first courses I played was a short, nine-hole, par 3 layout that was one of three courses in a nearby public golf facility. The holes range from 100 yards to 200 yards. The practice facility also has a driving range and I soon discovered that I could leave my office shortly after noon, wolf down a sandwich in the car, spend thirty minutes hitting balls on the range and then play two or three balls on the par 3 course (which was always deserted in the early afternoon during the week), and be back in my office by 2:30. In a little over two hours, including travel time, I had hit 100 balls on the range, played the equivalent of twenty-seven holes of golf, and gotten a fair amount of exercise. My game improved rapidly, I lost weight, and I had a lot of fun in the process.

Such a routine may not be possible for everyone. The important lesson is to be creative in searching for ways to practice your game.

How to Find Practice Facilities

Local clubs and facilities

If you don't belong to a golf or country club that has an adequate practice facility, you will have to search for one (or more) where you can work on your game. Most areas have directories of local clubs and courses: public, semi-public, resort, and private. If practice facilities are not described, a phone call to the pro shop will provide the information you need, including type of facilities available, cost, and hours they are open. You can then try out the facilities, beginning with the most convenient. You may discover that there is a nearby driving range, but that you will have to travel farther for a complete practice facility.

Practice and instruction

We talk about the things to look for in choosing a golf teacher in "Resources" at the back of the book, but one important consideration is whether your teacher is located at a club that has a good practice facility. If so, you may well be eligible for discounts on the range and you can combine practice with instruction more easily.

Golf schools and major practice facilities

Scattered across the country, especially in resort areas that emphasize golf, are hundreds of golf schools, resorts, and other complexes, most of which offer very complete practice facilities. A few days or longer spent at or near one of these facilities can do wonders for your game, whether you take lessons or not. While the golf courses associated with these facilities usually are very expensive to play, the practice facilities often are a real bargain (sometimes free). An example is Marriott's Shadow Ridge Resort in Desert Springs, California. It costs more than $100 per person to play the Shadow Ridge golf course in season, but only $20 per day for unlimited use of a world-class practice facility. See the resources section at the back of this book for a list of other golf schools and resorts that have great practice facilities.

Practice bunkers at the PGA Learning Center in Port St. Lucie, Florida

Backswings

- It is virtually impossible to improve your golf skills without practice.
- The quality of your practice is as important as the quantity.
- Find ways to practice at home.
- Practice all of the important skills—the full swing, chipping, pitching, bunker play, and putting.
- Develop a practice routine.
- Incorporate games into your routine.
- Remember to practice on the golf course.
- Don't overdo it.

Chapter 4

Equipment

*Golf is a game whose aim is to hit a very small ball into a very
small hole with weapons singularly ill-suited for the purpose.*
—Winston Churchill

Golf is a sport in which participation requires a fair amount
of specialized equipment, principally golf clubs, but also balls, a
bag to carry the clubs, and a variety of other accessories, including shoes and gloves. Getting the right equipment is comparable
to bicycling, mountain climbing, hunting or fishing, and camp-
ing. As in each of these sports, advances in technology have dramatically increased the equipment choices available to participants, with some important implications for older golfers. Let's
start with the basics.

Choosing Golf Clubs

If you are taking up the game for the first time, the first thing you need is some golf clubs. Until you have taken some lessons, practiced a few times on the range, and begin to have a sense of your level of interest and commitment to the game, you should borrow or rent clubs instead of purchasing them. If you are getting back into the game after a period away from it, drag your old clubs out of the closet and don't rush out to buy a new set until you know how your body and your skills have changed since you last played.

When you are first learning how to swing a golf club, you may only need one or two clubs: probably a lofted wood, such as a 5- or 7-fairway wood and a mid-range iron, such as a 7-iron. These two clubs will give you a feel for the differences between irons and woods and you won't have to learn to compensate for the variations in length among five or six different clubs. When you begin to feel that you have some control over these two clubs and can get the ball into the air some of the time, you can think about purchasing a set of clubs.

Advice from the Pro
What's in the Bag?

A typical set of golf clubs contains a putter, a number of irons (made of steel heads, with steel or graphite shafts), and several woods (once upon a time the heads were made out of wood, but now all are manufactured in metal alloys, such as titanium, but we still call them "woods"). Irons and woods vary both in length and loft (the angle of the club face which determines the trajectory of the ball when it is hit). Longer clubs are designed to hit the ball farther because of greater leverage and a lower trajectory;

shorter, higher-lofted clubs are designed to produce a higher trajectory. Irons vary in length from club to club in ½-inch increments.

Complete sets of irons usually consist of numbers 3 through 9, plus at least a pitching wedge, a sand wedge, and often an additional wedge or two. (Wedges have a pronounced loft.) The entire set of irons is usually matched (same flexes in shafts and ½-inch increments in length). A set of woods may be included with the irons, or they may have to be purchased separately. A set of woods typically includes a driver (1-wood), 3-wood, 5-wood, and perhaps a 7-wood or 9-wood. The rules of golf allow golfers to carry a maximum of fourteen clubs in their bag and many golfers are replacing their long irons with lofted woods (usually a 7-wood or 9-wood) and/or hybrid clubs (a cross between a wood and an iron), which are easier to hit. —Mary Beth

Everyone agrees that novice golfers should avoid spending a lot of money on a first set of clubs. As your game improves, you will have a better idea of your personal preferences and needs and will have some basis for navigating the bewildering array of possibilities, including whether you should have clubs specially fitted for you. In the interim, Mary Beth recommends that beginning golfers carry a modified set of clubs, consisting of the following:

- a putter,
- four irons (5, 7, and 9, and a pitching wedge or sand wedge), and
- two woods (a 3-wood to use as a driving club and a high-lofted fairway wood or hybrid to hit from the fairway).

*From left: driver, fairway wood,
7-iron, pitching wedge*

Such a collection of clubs avoids the most difficult clubs to hit (the long irons and the driver) and takes account of the fact that it takes some time before most new golfers are able to see much of a difference between adjacent clubs; for example, between the 7- and 8-irons. Additional advantages are that it is easier to decide which club to hit when you have fewer clubs and seven clubs weigh a lot less than the twelve to fourteen clubs in a full set. Many older golfers may never need more clubs than this partial starter set.

Advice from the Pro
Getting a Modified Set of Clubs

Irons are usually sold in complete, matched sets. If you aren't able to borrow a few clubs from a friend or relative when you take up the game, it may be more economical to purchase a full set and carry only the clubs you wish to carry in the beginning. If you and a friend are learning to play at the same time, splitting a set of irons between the two of you may work for a while. Note, however, that golf courses usually require each player to have a golf bag. —Mary Beth

Whether you begin with a full or partial set of clubs, older golfers should make sure that their clubs have flexible shafts to help compensate for their slower swing speeds. The most flexible men's shafts are labeled "light" or "A" or "Senior," depending on the manufacturer. Standard women's clubs typically are one inch shorter than men's clubs, and they have smaller-sized grips and even more flexible shafts.

To fit or not to fit?

As your game improves, you will know when it is time to expand your arsenal of clubs, either one at a time, or by purchasing a full set. When you can't find a club in your bag that enables you to hit balls a certain distance, you will be in the market for new or additional clubs to fill in the gaps in your game. At this point, you may decide to have clubs custom fitted to meet the requirements of your individual characteristics. Great strides have been made in the manufacture of custom-fitted clubs, and both men and women over 50 are among the major beneficiaries. Custom-fitted clubs can vary in length, shaft flex, grip size, head size and design, and lie angles for irons, and they take into account individual variations in height; weight; length of arms, legs, or torso; hand and palm sizes; and strength. Individuals who have particular physical characteristics or limitations, such as arthritis, also may benefit greatly by using custom-fitted clubs.

How much difference do clubs make?

One day, I joined a foursome on my local public course that included a very athletic-looking guy in his mid-thirties who, it soon turned out, was an accomplished golfer. This was the first time that I had seen anyone hit the ball 250 yards or more, straight down the fairway every time he swung his driver and I was impressed. After watching him roll the ball into the hole for his third straight par, I happened to notice the clubs in his bag. His woods were made of wood. And, if this wasn't enough, his irons all had wooden shafts. When I expressed my astonishment at the clubs he was using, he smiled and said that these were his *grandfather's* clubs and that he had been playing with them since he was a teenager. When I asked why he hadn't acquired new clubs, he replied: "I learned to play with these clubs, I'm used to them, and I don't see any reason to replace them."

As the golf industry has pushed the use of advanced technology and materials in the manufacture of new clubs, it has also perfected the art of advertising to its consumers. Whenever I pick up a new issue of *Golf Magazine,* I find it difficult to resist jumping in my car and heading for the nearest golf store to buy a new club or set of clubs that is guaranteed to eliminate my slices and hooks and add dozens of yards to every shot. And, each set of clubs *looks* more powerful and beautiful than the one before it. Alas, while there is no doubt that there have been important technological advances in club design and manufacture, under any circumstances clubs only account for a small portion of the variation in performance on the golf course. No matter what exotic alloy is used in a club's manufacture or how sophisticated the weighting system designed to compensate for hooks and slices, the two main factors in how far the ball travels after it is hit are the speed of the clubhead at impact and how squarely the club strikes the ball.

Any new clubs, moreover, take some time to learn how to hit. It is unlikely, therefore, that any new club or set of clubs will automatically fix whatever problems you have with your swing or increase significantly the distance you can hit the ball, especially in the short term. However, they may make you *feel* better and that can be worth far more than the price you pay for them.

How expensive are golf clubs?
Like almost anything else, individual golf clubs and sets of clubs

New Clubs—The Excitement
of the Latest Technology

Buying a new club (or set of clubs) is an important part of the sport for many golfers. I have a friend who loves to spend time at the local golf store and often comes home with a new driver, fairway wood, hybrid, or putter and, every now and then, a whole new set of irons. Each new club holds out the possibility that it will enable him to hit shots he couldn't hit before. Whether the new clubs improve his game in the long run is less important to him than the excitement of trying the new technology.

vary widely in price. You can find complete sets of clubs, including a bag to put them in, for under $300 at many discount stores. One of these sets might be your best bet when you are taking up the game, though most such package deals are for clubs fitted with regular-flex shafts. Sooner or later, you will be in the market for a set of clubs that is better suited to your strength and abilities.

At the other extreme, you can easily spend $300 or $500 for a new driver, $150 for a putter, and $900 or more for a matched set of irons. If you have figured out what clubs you want (with the advice of your teacher, by trying your friends' clubs, or through visits to golf stores), you can often cut the cost in half by purchasing used clubs. Several of the major manufacturers have websites where they offer pre-owned but completely reconditioned clubs, both individually and in sets. I have purchased several clubs this way at steeply discounted prices, and I could not tell that the clubs I received in the mail had ever been used.

What clubs should be in *your* bag?

Even given the constraints of a traditional set of golf clubs, the range of choices available today for golfers of all ages and skill levels is enormous. Add to this array the new hybrids and redesigned fairway woods, and the task of choosing the right set of clubs to match any individual's particular set of skills can be a challenge. Part of the fun of golf is experimenting with different clubs and configurations of clubs in your bag. As you do so, it is important to remember that accuracy and consistency are more important than distance in almost every situation. The following are a few things to think about as you choose your weapons.

- Like many older men and women, I have replaced my long irons (my 3-iron and 4-iron) with new lofted fairway woods (a 7 and 11) and a hybrid (combination wood and iron) that, at least for me, are much easier to hit. I now use these clubs for all shots over 140 yards. *Golf Magazine* recently ran a series of articles about using a hybrid for four different shots, including both chipping and hitting off the tee. This is one area where advances in technology really have made a big difference for older golfers. I still carry 6-, 7-, 8-, and 9-irons, along with three wedges, including a pitching wedge, a sand wedge, and a lob (highly lofted) wedge.
- The driver is the longest and most difficult club to hit consistently, despite all of the hoopla about the forgiveness of larger clubheads and bigger sweet spots. Unless you are able to hit it well, a driver won't give you extra yards off the tee. (Even Tiger Woods often uses a 3-wood instead of his driver to provide better control.) If you are determined to buy a driver, look for one with more loft, at least twelve or thirteen degrees, and select the most flexible shaft. Be prepared to practice a lot with it before you use it in prime time and bring extra balls for those occasions when you hook or slice your tee shot into the woods.

• The putter accounts for 40 percent of your score, and therefore, it is the most important club in your bag. There are a lot of new putters on the market that incorporate significant technological advances and it is worth spending some time experimenting with different styles both on the course and on the practice putting green (or in your living room at home). Many courses with pro shops will let you try out several putters on the practice green.

• Finally, keep reminding yourself of the guy I mentioned earlier who used his grandfather's wooden clubs. In spite of all the technological advances in the construction of golf clubs, by far the most important variable always will be the person swinging the club.

Golf Balls

Golf balls are obviously pretty important, too, and their construction also has been influenced in significant ways by technological developments in the last few decades. Like golf clubs, there is now a wide array of balls to choose from, with considerable variation in price, but, unfortunately, less differentiation in performance. The construction of golf balls is regulated by the USGA and the challenge faced by all ball manufacturers is how to make balls that conform to the rules of golf regarding size, weight, velocity and maximum distance and yet appeal to golfers of differing abilities. Golf balls differ from each other in the following four major ways:

• *Cost.* Balls are constructed in one of three ways: two pieces, three pieces, and four pieces. In general, two-piece balls are much less expensive than three-piece and four-piece balls, their covers are thicker and therefore more durable, and tests show that they travel just as far off the tee as more expensive balls. *They are just as white.* The majority of all golfers use two-piece balls.

• *Feel.* High compression balls feel harder when hit than lower compression balls, which are advertised as having a "softer feel." Lower compression balls are better suited for golfers with slower swing speeds, including most older men and women, in terms of both feel and distance. Feel, however, is a matter of personal preference and you can find golf balls with a softer feel in all price ranges.

• *Spin.* Expert golfers want a ball that spins when they hit it. Spinning the ball enables them to control the ball's flight and what it does when it lands. The shots you see pros make that bend around trees and then bounce backward when they land on the green require such a ball. Most three-piece and four-piece balls are easier to spin, and they are therefore the choice of professionals. For us duffers, increased spin more often than not only exacerbates our mistakes.

• *Accuracy.* In *Consumer Reports'* tests, most three-piece and four-piece balls were slightly more accurate when hit by robots, both off the driver and with an 8-iron. If you can find a robot to hit your tee shots for you, these balls might be a good choice. Otherwise, my recommendation is to stick to the less expensive, more durable balls that travel just as far when you hit them.

Having confidence in your ball

Most golfers, myself included, develop preferences over time for one brand of golf ball over another. Extensive testing done by organizations ranging from *Golf Magazine* to *Consumer Reports* does not provide much support for such preferences. In my experience, however, *feeling good* about my choice of golf ball is an extremely important determinant of whether I hit it well or not. I think that I hit some kinds of golf balls better than others, and anything that increases my confidence is good. When I miss a shot with another brand, I can always blame the ball for my mistake.

When to open that sleeve of new balls

For many golfers, opening a sleeve of new balls (golf balls usually come in boxes of three, called a "sleeve") when they arrive at the first tee is one of the pleasurable rituals in any round of golf. The new balls are pristine, shiny, and embody all of the hopes and expectations that dance in one's head before the first shot. This feeling is guaranteed to last at least until you take your first swing at the ball.

Other golfers root around in their golf bag, looking for the ball they brought back from their last successful round, hoping that it retains the aura of good luck that it held yesterday or last week, notwithstanding its nicks and scuff marks. More often than not, I find myself in this latter category. While I appreciate the pleasure of using new golf balls, I have lost too many new balls in the woods for me to fully trust a new ball. I prefer to carry the new ball in my right hand pocket and put it into play only when I lose my tried-and-true ball. There have been periods where I happily played with the same scuffed up ball for a couple of weeks, while the new ball remained in my pocket.

One of the important lessons I draw from my avowedly superstitious behavior is that confidence in the ability to hit the ball is more important than its age or construction. Like most golfers, I will, on average, continue to lose a ball or two (if not more) each time I play, and I will continue to spend my share of the more than $700 million spent on golf balls in this country each year. However, most of us could probably get along fine using the lost balls we find every day on the course that someone else paid for, especially when we find our favorite brand.

The Golf Bag

You have the essentials—clubs and balls—and now you need something to carry them in. Your new clubs may have come with a golf bag, in which case you can skip this section. If not, the following are a few tips about golf bag selection.

- Even if you never plan on carrying your bag (on your back) on the golf course, you still have to lift it and your clubs in and out of your car and move it around your garage. So, think about how much it will weigh when fully loaded with clubs, a dozen balls, a sweater and rain jacket, a sandwich, and a bottle of water.

• Some bags come equipped with legs that extend out automatically when you set the bag down (not surprisingly, these are called "stand bags"). This type of bag is essential if you plan to walk and carry your clubs on the course. If you expect that you will always ride in a power cart when you play or use a pull cart (see below), you may not need a stand bag and the legs may turn out be more of a nuisance than an advantage, especially when strapping the bag to the back of a power cart. Your bag must have a comfortable shoulder strap in any case, preferably a dual strap that distributes the weight on your back, like a backpack.

• While weight is a factor, remember that your bag has to accommodate all the things you need for the better part of a day on the course under a variety of conditions. It must have several sturdy pockets of various sizes that are easy to get at and to open and close. It should have a place to attach a towel and perhaps a small bag that holds your tees and other small tools. When you use a power cart, make sure your bag is positioned on the back of the cart in such a way that you have easy access to the things you need.

• Every bag should have a detachable rain cover. Even if your bag is on a golf cart, you need to protect your clubs from the rain and keep the bag from filling up with water.

A Pull or Push Cart

One of the reasons I play golf is for exercise. Walking nine or even eighteen holes on a nice day is a great experience and it is good for you, to boot. Carrying my bag and clubs on my back is another matter. Like many older adults, I have from time to time had problems with my lower back, and I work very hard to make sure that these problems don't reoccur. Picking up and putting down twenty pounds of equipment approximately eighty times during my round of golf isn't part of my exercise program. Yet, unless a course is particularly long (with long distances between holes) or hilly, I much prefer walking to riding in a golf cart.

The solution to this problem is a pull or push cart designed to transport your golf bag, including your clubs and other equipment. Many even include a device to hold a water or soda bottle. Constructed out of aluminum, they are durable, very light, and easy to push ahead of you or pull behind you. Some are equipped with electric motors and some even have remote controls, so you don't even have to push or pull them. Most cost between $50 and $100, and I regard my pull cart as one of the best investments I have made since I took up the game of golf. Most of my friends feel the same way.

I should note that some serious golfers look down on the pull cart set. In their view, carrying one's clubs on one's back is part of the game. And, there are a few golf courses that prohibit pull carts on the course, whether to ensure increased revenue from power cart rentals or because of legitimate concerns about maintaining the pace of play.

What to Wear

Despite today's greater informality in standards of dress, virtually all golf clubs require golfers to wear a shirt with a collar and sleeves. Golf shorts are acceptable almost everywhere. Many courses do not permit jeans. If you have any doubts about dress requirements at any club, call the pro shop and inquire. (On one occasion, I called a golf club in Johannesburg, South Africa, to ask whether I could use the practice facility and was told that, in addition to a collared shirt, white socks were required if I wore shorts.)

Shoes

Many golfers choose to wear golf shoes with soft plastic spikes on the soles for better traction. They come in many styles and colors. Some look like sneakers; others look like wing tip dress shoes. With most golf shoes, the spikes can be replaced when they wear down. Steel spikes are no longer permitted at most courses because they can cause too much damage to the greens.

Gloves and hats

Most professionals and recreational golfers wear a specially designed leather or synthetic material golf glove on their left hand (if they play right-handed). Its purpose is to improve your grip on the club with the hand that is responsible for leading your swing and to help absorb vibration when you don't hit the ball cleanly. It is not required, but it helps us older folks to hang on to our clubs at the end of our swing. Pros usually take them off when they putt for improved feel in their hands. No one I play with does this.

Baseball caps or visors help keep the sun out of your eyes and keep you cooler in the summer. I have a friend who wears a straw hat when it's really hot because it permits more air flow than tighter-fitting caps. He also wears a white golf shirt to deflect the sun.

Sunglasses and sunscreen

Even if you don't routinely wear sunglasses, they can be very useful in helping to see where your ball goes, particularly when you are playing into the sun. Also, they protect your eyes from dangerous UV rays. Sunscreen with a high UV rating is highly recommended. Put in on well in advance, so your hands are not sticky.

Rain gear

You should always carry a light rain jacket in your golf bag, even if the day is bright and sunny. A sudden change in the weather is always possible, and if you don't keep a rain jacket in your bag all the time, it won't be there when you need it. Obviously, an umbrella is useful if it rains.

Layers in winter

Once you've been bitten by the golf bug, you are likely to want to play in all sorts of weather. It's difficult to play in snow, even with a brightly colored ball, and golf courses close when greens are frozen or have frost or snow on them. Many courses close when there is too much water on the course. Short of these extremes, you are likely to find courses open most of the year. Cooler weather is an especially good time to walk, as opposed to riding in a power cart, because walking helps to keep you warm. Dress in layers and expect to shed them as you play. Pick up a pair of winter golf gloves to keep your hands warm.

For about $100, you can purchase a large plastic cover that fits over any standard golf cart. It will keep the wind out when it's cold, and if the sun is out, it will keep you toasty warm between shots. You can even find small propane heaters that fit into the cup holder. Who said it's too cold for a round of golf?

Essential Tools

In addition to your clubs and golf balls, there are a few other things you need in your golf bag.

Tees

The only really inexpensive things that are integral to the game of golf are tees, the things you stick in the ground to hold your ball up for the first shot at each hole. They may be made of plastic or wood (even corn), and they come in different lengths, shapes and colors. Since they break about half the time when you hit the ball off of them, it's a good thing they are cheap. Experiment with the different types and decide which you like best. I have always stuck with the standard, medium length, wooden tee. Put a handful in your pocket at the first hole, so you don't have to get one out of your bag each time you tee off. They can also be used in your backyard for practicing your swing, without a ball.

If you play during the winter, it is useful to have a few tees in your bag that are designed to sit on top of the ground instead of penetrating it, for use when the ground is frozen solid.

Green repair tool

When balls land on the green, especially if they have been hit from some distance away or high in the air, they usually make a mark (often a deep gouge). Golfers are expected to repair such marks using a special tool that you should always carry in your bag and put into your pocket at the beginning of your round. Get someone to show you the proper way to use this tool to repair ball marks the first time you are on a course. If you forget or lose your tool, a golf tee will do in a pinch.

Ball marker

Your pocket should also contain a coin or two, or some other type of ball marker to use in marking the position of your ball on the green when it is in the path of another golfer's putt, or when you pick up the ball to clean it before putting. Don't forget to pick up your marker and put it back into your pocket after you place your ball back down on the green. Many golf gloves have a marker attached to them, but unless you get into the habit of using it and then replacing it onto your glove, it will soon be lost.

Towel

You should attach a towel to the outside of your bag with which to clean and dry your golf balls and your clubs. Most golf towels have a grommet and one of those hooks designed to hang shower curtains with which you can attach it to the bag.

Ball retriever

It is very useful to carry a telescoping ball retriever in your bag for those occasions when your ball ends up in a pond or stream, or just out of reach under a bush.

Wire brush for cleaning clubs

It is also useful to clip a small wire brush onto your bag to use to clean dirt out of the grooves in your clubs. You can always use your fingernail or a tee, like I sometimes do, but a brush works better. The grooves in your clubs impart spin to the ball and they don't work as well when they are full of dirt.

Pencils and paper

It's a good idea to keep two or three small pencils with erasers in your bag, along with a notebook, not only to keep score, but also to make notes on the course and record any other statistics you are keeping track of. A notebook is also handy to take notes during your lessons.

Advice from the Pro
Don't Forget Practice Aids

In addition to the things you need on the course, the following items will make it easier to practice at home or in a nearby park.

- A small artificial turf mat—to practice chipping and pitching without tearing up your lawn.
- A plastic tube used to pick up balls—to save your back when you practice.
- A basket for used balls—to hold your collection of practice balls.
- A few dozen plastic balls—for practicing your swing without breaking windows.
- A short, weighted club—for practicing your swing indoors and loosening up before a round.

—Mary Beth

Golf as a Gift Opportunity

Finally, my wife reminds me that the gear of golf provides a never-ending source of gift opportunities and ideas for friends and family. With a golfer in the family, the problem of what to give the person who has everything vanishes because he or she always can use another golf shirt, or dozen golf balls, or glove, or training aid, not to mention a gift certificate for lessons or a round of golf at a favorite golf club or resort. Enjoy.

Backswings

- Equipment is less important than the person using it.
- Don't buy expensive golf balls.
- New technology is fun, but it probably won't cure your slice.
- Resist the urge to play with a driver until you can hit it consistently on the practice range.
- Substitute a new hybrid club and/or high-lofted fairway woods for the long irons (3–5) in your bag.
- Buy a pull cart if you plan to walk any time, instead of riding in a power cart.

Chapter 5

Making Yourself at Home
on the Golf Course

*Since bad shots come in groups of three, a fourth bad shot is
actually the beginning of the next group of three.*

One of the things that inhibited me from learning to play
golf is that I didn't really know much about what it's like to be
on a golf course. Of course, I had *seen* golf courses, on television
and out of the window of my room during occasional stays at
resort hotels. I had glimpsed golf courses from the highway and
while attending wedding receptions at one of the local country
clubs. However, I hadn't actually been on a course with a golf
club in my hand and the whole enterprise remained something
of a mystery.

In the first place, it was difficult to imagine how *big* a golf course actually is until I had walked or driven in a golf cart on one from beginning to end. Most 18-hole courses are between 6,500 and 7,200 yards long from the back tees, more than three and a half miles, and that's not counting the distance between each green and the location of the next tee (which can add another mile or so on some courses). Second, every course is unique and because each of the 18 holes is designed to be more or less self-contained—often screened by trees or other physical features from the other holes on the course—there is no single place to get a perspective of the whole course unless you are in a helicopter, airplane, or hot air balloon. Even if you could see the whole course from above, you wouldn't gain much of a sense of either the aesthetics of the environment or the challenges of playing the game itself. Each hole is a surprise, like opening a birthday present, the first time you arrive at the teeing area.

On the golf course

Finally, I didn't know much about the rules of the game, not to mention golf etiquette. Watching a golf tournament on television simply doesn't do it. The logistics of organizing a round of golf, choosing a place to play, reserving a tee time, getting to the course, and dealing with the formalities of paying for your round and renting a golf cart can be intimidating for the beginner.

This chapter provides information to help you become comfortable on any golf course as quickly as possible. The sooner you can stop worrying about whether to tip the bag boy and how to get to the first tee, the sooner you can start worrying about hitting your ball into the woods.

If you've played golf before, you can skip the next section. If you've only played a few rounds and are looking forward to spending more time on the links, read on.

The First Time

I'll assume that you have taken a few lessons, spent some time on a driving range, and managed to acquire a set of golf clubs. If you haven't gotten to the point where you have some confidence in your ability to hit an occasional decent shot on the range, I urge you not to set foot on a golf course unless you are accompanied by a teaching professional. Resist your friends' entreaties to join them, especially when they tell you how tolerant they will be of your beginner status. It will not speed your learning or contribute to your budding enthusiasm for the game to spend a couple of hours missing shot after shot in front of your friends or colleagues, no matter what they say.

However, if your golf teacher proposes to take you out onto the course for an actual playing lesson, this is a horse of a different color. My first experience on a golf course was under the tutelage of my coauthor, Mary Beth McGirr. Though I was still a rank beginner, the opportunity to experience what it is like to play golf in the company of someone who is highly skilled, extremely knowledgeable and personally supportive is, as the saying goes, priceless. No golf professional will take a beginner out on a course for a teaching round on a busy Saturday or Sunday, nor will they likely take someone who has not had some experience swinging a club. When your teacher thinks you are ready, however, he or she can arrange a tee time when the course is not busy. Mary Beth walked us through the process of paying for our greens fees, renting a power cart, loading our golf bags onto the cart, and getting the starter's permission to proceed to the first tee. In the process, she made sure we had, in addition to our golf clubs, the necessary accessories, including tees, a scorecard, and a repair tool for the greens.

Mary Beth played along with us for nine holes and, in addition to pointing out the main features of the course, demonstrated what it's like to hit really good shots: graceful and seemingly effortless swings that sent her ball high and far to land gently near her target. Watching her play was at least as valuable as the instruction we received on strategy, etiquette, and course management. I came away discouraged by my inability to hit the ball, but inspired by what I hoped might lie ahead. Having a clear vision of what the game of golf can be helped to sustain my motivation to practice and play during the time it takes to "get over the hump," that is, to develop enough skills so that the game becomes truly enjoyable. A good first experience on the course can go a long way toward creating such a vision.

What the Game of Golf Can Be: Strategy, Not Fear

The best vision of what the game of golf can be starts with two related capacities, one physical and one psychological: *control and confidence.* When a golfer gets to the point where he is reasonably confident that, *within the limits of his strength and skills,* he can hit the ball where he wants to hit it *most of the time,* the game suddenly changes. No longer is your first thought, "Will I miss this shot?" It is, "Where and how do I want to hit this shot?" Everyone flubs shots, but when strategy replaces fear, golf becomes the game we all imagine it might be.

The following are my suggestions about your first time on a golf course:

- Don't venture forth to play with other golfers until you have had a few lessons and spent enough time on a driving range to begin to have confidence that you can hit at least an occasional good shot. Depending on your ability and physical shape, this might be three or four lessons and a few hours on the range. Or, it might be a lot more.
- If possible, when you feel you are ready, arrange to play all or part of your first round with a (supportive) teaching professional. Your first experience might be only a few holes; it should not be more than nine.
- However, if your first experience is with friends or family, try to avoid any time when the course is likely to be crowded. Whatever format you and your friends play, don't keep track of your score. Bring lots of extra (preferably used) balls. Beware of playing with your spouse unless you are both beginners and can resist giving each other advice and/or criticism.
- I strongly recommend that you do *not* play with strangers the first time out.

Where Should (Can) You Play?

There are more than 10,000 golf courses in the United States and Canada that are open to the public (and, of course, many more throughout the world). These include municipal courses, privately owned courses that are open to the public, and courses that are part of resorts. Many new courses are being built each year, many of them associated with residential developments, including retirement communities. In addition, there are roughly 4,000 member-only courses, most of them at country clubs.

Private golf clubs

If you already belong to, or decide to join a country club, all of your initial golfing needs will be taken care of by the resident pro, who will organize lessons, encourage you to practice, and help arrange play with other members who are more or less at your skill level. Your club will become your "home course," and you will rapidly become familiar with all of the major features and eccentricities of the golf course. When you are ready to establish a handicap, you will do it through your club. Depending on how serious you are about golf, you may eventually participate in the many tournaments and other activities organized as part of the club's golf program. Your club is likely to have reciprocal relationships with other private clubs that enable you to play their courses (although the clubs you visit will most certainly charge you greens fees and cart rental costs).

Country clubs typically require an initial membership fee (which may be partially or entirely refundable when you leave) and annual dues that may cover part or all of the use of the club's facilities, including the golf course. Some clubs require that members spend a minimum amount on dining and other services each month. Some of the most exclusive clubs have waiting lists, and both membership fees and annual dues can be expensive.

Your choice of a private club, if you decide to go this route, likely will be determined by many factors, in addition to characteristics of the golf course. The rest of this section is predicated on the assumption that you will spend some of your time at public or semipublic courses, at least at the beginning of your relationship with golf.

Public courses
Every golf course is different and playing a new course is an important part of the fun and challenge of golf. In addition to lower costs, one advantage of playing on public courses is that you are likely to have many choices of when and where to play and learn. Given these riches, how do you decide where to play?

At the beginning, convenience and the availability of a practice facility, including, at a minimum, a putting green and a driving range, were my primary considerations. I knew I would be less likely to practice if I couldn't get to the range easily and my progress would be much slower. I took my first lessons at a nearby local municipal course, which has a large driving range, including heated stalls for winter practice. There are three golf courses in the complex: two nine-hole courses and one 18-hole layout. One of the nine-hole courses consists entirely of par 3 holes, and it was a perfect place not only to begin playing, but also to practice my short game as my skills improved. Although crowded on weekends, all three courses are readily accessible without advanced tee times during the week. Ease of getting on the course is another important consideration in choosing places to play, especially if the time you have available for golf is limited.

Next on the list of things to consider is the difficulty of the golf course. Golf courses vary greatly in difficulty and when you are starting out, it is really discouraging to tackle a course that is designed for experts. The municipal courses near my home are relatively easy courses and that made a big difference to me in the beginning. It still does when I am in need of a confidence-building experience.

The things that make a course more difficult include the following:

- Narrow fairways and sloped fairways, bordered by trees and/or difficult rough (very long grass), requiring accurate tee shots and/or the ability to hit your ball out of the rough when you miss the fairway.
- Numerous bunkers, both on the fairways and surrounding the greens (bunkers also vary greatly in how difficult they are to hit out of).
- Hazards, including water and other physical features such as bushes and very tall grass, that can either swallow your ball or lead to unplayable lies.
- Holes that require blind shots (often due to doglegs) or shots that must travel over or around obstacles on the course.
- Hilly terrain, especially if you will have to hit shots off of ground that is not level.

- Greens that make putts difficult because of their slope(s), speed, and pin placements.
  - The length of the course.

You can determine the difficulty of any course by going to its web page (if it doesn't have a web page, call the pro shop and ask) and looking at three sets of numbers that will be posted: the *yardage* from each of the course's three to five sets of tees and the *course* and *slope ratings* for each set of tees. We will have more to say about the tees you should play from in the chapter on course management. Course and slope ratings are explained in the sidebar "How Difficult Is the Course" that follows. Suffice it to say here, if you are taking up the game over the age of 50, you are likely to have more fun (translation: less frustration and aggravation) playing on courses and from tees with lower slope ratings. If you do decide to play a more challenging course, at least you'll know to bring extra balls.

After convenience, availability of a practice facility, accessibility, and difficulty, the following factors may enter into the decision about where to play:

- How much it costs (see the section below for tips on saving money).
  - How well maintained the course is and how likely is it to be affected by recent weather (for example, is there likely to be standing water caused by recent thunderstorms?).
  - Whether golfers are permitted to walk or whether rental of a power cart is required.
  - Whether power carts are restricted to cart paths, or not.
  - How attractive and interesting the course is.
  - And, of course, where your friends want to play.

Choosing a golf course is like picking a restaurant. As I gained experience playing different courses, I developed favorites that I return to again and again. At the same time, every new course is an adventure (just like a new restaurant), and there is always the possibility that I will discover a new favorite. On occasion, I decide to splurge on an expensive, highly rated, famous course, just for the experience, even though my scores on such courses typically have been dismal. When I travel with the family, new courses are an important part of the experience. When we return home, the familiarity of the old standby is comforting and I usually play better there, too.

How Difficult Is the Course?

All officially registered golf courses in the United States are inspected by a team of USGA certified raters (who are accomplished amateurs). Two ratings for each set of tees are assigned. These ratings are measures of the course's difficulty when played from those tee boxes. The closer (shorter) sets of tees are usually rated separately for men and women.

Course rating. The course rating is the average score for 18 holes that a professional golfer would make when playing from each set of tees. These ratings reflect the course's difficulty for expert players.

Slope rating. The slope rating is a measure of the course's difficulty for average* players, reflecting the fact that scores of average players rise more quickly than scores of experts as the difficulty of the course increases (hence the term "slope"). Slope ratings range from 55–155, with an average slope being 113. The higher the number, the more difficult the course for average players.

Example: Twin Lakes, Clifton, Virginia—Lakes Course

Tees	Rating/Slope		Tees	Rating/Slope	
Blue:	71.7/124		Gold:	Men	67.7/115
				Ladies	72.9/126
White:	69.6/122				
			Red:	Ladies	69.9/108

These numbers show that, except for women playing from the red tees (slope rating of 108), this course is more difficult than average for average players. A professional golfer playing from the white tees would score on average 69.6, slightly better than par. The slope rating of 122 from the white tees means that average players will tend to score higher than their usual scores. Beginners will find this course to be a challenge.

Average male players score between 95 and 100.
Average female players post scores between 105 and 110.

Who should you play with?

During my first few times on a golf course, I played with a pro, supportive friends, my spouse, or by myself (when I could find a nearly empty course). *My primary goals in the early stages were to get as many repetitions as possible, sustain my enthusiasm for the game, and have fun.*

As my confidence in my abilities began to grow, the range of people with whom I felt comfortable playing expanded quickly. I was pleasantly surprised to discover how many friends and acquaintances played golf and how easy it was to find someone to play golf with, often on a moment's notice. One of the unexpected pleasures of the game has been playing with people I knew, but had not spent much time with before golf. I also discovered that even on weekends I could walk on to almost any public course as a single and in most cases be welcomed as part of a compatible foursome, often without waiting more than a few minutes. Remarkably, I have never had a bad experience playing with people I met for the first time on the first tee. On top of all this, there have been opportunities to participate in organized leagues and occasional tournaments, and to add new people to my list of golfing partners. Finally, I continue to take delight in playing by myself when one of my home courses is deserted on a hot afternoon in summer or a cold morning in mid-winter.

Playing with People Who Are Better (or Worse) than You

Although it can be very competitive, golf is one of the few sports that can be played by people of varying skill levels at the same time. That's why individuals have handicaps and courses have different tee boxes to accommodate men and women of different abilities. Moreover, golfers are by necessity tolerant of mistakes made by other players in their foursome. They know that on the next hole they may be the one who hits a bad shot. One of the most important discoveries I made after I began playing golf is that the vast majority of golfers are not very much better, or are worse, than I am.

At the extremes, however, differences in abilities can put strains on the system. If a player typically needs six or seven shots to play most par 4 holes, golfers who shoot bogey golf (an average of only one over par on each hole) or better will have to wait while the less skilled player hits one or two extra shots on every hole. And, that's not taking into account time spent searching for balls hit into the trees or deep rough. Under such circumstances, it is impossible for the slower player to avoid detracting from the more experienced player's enjoyment of the game. Bottom line: As a relative newcomer to the game, I try not to play with golfers who are much better than I am, unless they are very good friends.

Nine or Eighteen Holes?

I had been taking lessons, practicing, and playing golf for quite a long time before playing my first round of eighteen holes. I remember vividly finishing the front nine and looking forward to taking a break for a leisurely lunch in the clubhouse, perhaps with a cold beer or glass of wine. I was dismayed to discover that if we stopped for lunch we would lose our place in the progression of foursomes on the course and might have to wait an hour or longer before there was a break in the schedule so we could get back onto the course. It turns out that almost no one ever interrupts play to eat. The best I could do was a hot dog snatched from the snack bar and wolfed down in the cart en route to the tenth hole.

Playing eighteen holes of golf requires a major commitment of time and energy. Even if there are no delays caused by slow players ahead of you, playing a full round of eighteen holes takes a minimum of four hours, not counting travel time to and from the golf club, hitting a few balls on the driving range and putting green, and dealing with formalities such as paying greens fees and renting a golf cart.

It also turns out to be much more tiring than I had expected. Even if you ride in a golf cart, there are a lot of physical demands, especially for people who haven't been particularly active. Moreover, I found that I wasn't used to sustaining the level of concentration necessary to keep hitting my best shots (no matter how poor they were relative to the others in my foursome) for such a long period of time.

Finally, the pace of golf turns out to be less relaxed than it appears when you watch it on television. Unless the course is unusually empty, there is constant pressure to keep moving so as not to keep the group behind waiting. This adds stress if you are hitting a lot of balls in places where you have to spend time searching for them, or if, like me, you simply require a lot of shots to get from tee to green.

My suggestions to combat fatigue and stress include the following:

- Don't feel you have to play eighteen holes every time you go to the course. Especially in the beginning, you may find that you get more enjoyment out of playing nine holes than you do playing eighteen. If so, stick to playing nine most of the time, as I do.

Play Now, Decide Later

At most golf clubs, when you pay your greens fees, the person in the pro shop will ask whether you want to play nine holes or eighteen holes. At many clubs, you don't have to decide at the beginning; pay for nine and they will give you a discount if you change your mind and decide to continue on after finishing the first nine.

• If you expect to play eighteen holes, plan your day so that you can enjoy the experience without feeling rushed. Arrive at the course early enough to warm up, hit some practice shots, pay your fees and get your equipment organized (this also applies even if you are only playing nine). Think about how you intend to stay hydrated and nourished during your round. Bring drinks and a sandwich, unless you are required to purchase them from the golf club (you can always stick a sandwich or an energy bar in a pocket of your golf bag before you leave home). Find out whether there is water on the course and if the concession cart will be operating while you are playing.

• Play on weekdays instead of on weekends if you can.

• Pace yourself. Especially if you are playing eighteen holes.

• Don't let a few poor shots on the first few holes get you down. There is always the back nine to look forward to.

• If it's hot, stay out of the sun as much as possible between shots.

• Don't allow yourself and your group to fall behind

the pace of play. Agree with your playing partners that you will drop a new ball if you can't find yours within a few minutes and that it is not necessary for everyone to help you look for your ball. Always carry one or two extra balls in your pocket.

Should You Walk or Ride?

Golf courses vary greatly in how difficult they are to walk. Some courses are hilly; some are relatively flat. The distance between holes on some courses is short; on others it can be a long walk. Aside from the characteristics of the course and your physical condition, the decision to ride or walk may depend on other factors, including the following:

• Some golf clubs require the use of a gas or electric cart (except, perhaps, in the off-season, during twilight hours, or at times when the course is less crowded than usual). In addition to increased revenue for the club, this rule often reflects the desire to ensure that golfers maintain the pace of play, due to the characteristics of the course itself, such as the distance between holes or the number of steep hills. I know one course that bans pull carts, but permits walkers after 2 P.M. if you carry your own clubs.

• When golf carts are restricted to cart paths only (for example, because the course is wet), the decision to walk or ride is sometimes more difficult. It is often easier and more efficient to walk down the center of the course than to walk back and forth across the course between your ball to where you parked your golf cart. Of course, you still have to carry your clubs or drag them behind you if you are walking.

• Power carts enable you to transport drinks, sandwiches, extra clothing, and any other equipment more easily than pull carts. Also, an increasing number of clubs are equipping their power carts with GPS systems that provide precise yardages from where your ball is situated to the hole; the knowledge of the precise distance to the hole from where your ball lies can be of great assistance in club selection.

Accommodations for Handicapped Golfers

Most golf courses are more than willing to make special accommodations for handicapped golfers. Special flags can be attached to golf carts that permit them to be driven on the course when all other carts are restricted to cart paths, and to park carts closer to the green for golfers who have difficulty walking. My father-in-law plays golf with a portable oxygen tank, and a friend's uncle Vito, despite being a paraplegic, manages just fine by propping himself up against the side of the cart in order to swing his club.

How Much Does It Cost? Are There Ways to Save Money?

Golf can be an expensive pastime. It costs a lot of money to build and maintain a golf course properly and to provide the kinds of amenities most golfers expect. These costs are reflected in greens fees at public courses or in initiation and annual membership fees at private clubs. In general, the better the course, the more meticulously it is maintained, the better the service, and the more elegant the amenities (clubhouse, restaurants, locker rooms, pro shop, etc.), the more it will cost to play. That said, at least for public golf clubs, there are a number of ways to save money.

- The single best way to save money is to avoid playing on weekends and during peak hours. It can cost twice as much to play golf on a weekend as during the week. However, on both weekdays and weekends, it usually costs less to play during "twilight hours" (depending on the course, twilight hours usually begin at early to mid-afternoon). If you only intend to play nine holes, a late afternoon tee time is often a good bet. (At my municipal course, some weekday rates go *up* after 2 P.M. because so many golfers play after work.)

- Many public courses offer special inducements to get golfers to play during the week. There is a course near me that offers a buffet breakfast *and* lunch, *and* golf cart rental for $29 for eighteen holes of play Monday through Thursday. If the cuisine were better, it would almost pay to go there just for the food.

- Most courses offer special rates to seniors who play during the week. In many areas, there are organized groups of golfers over 55 or 60 who play regularly at different courses during the week and use the power of numbers to negotiate lower group rates for their members. Some courses set aside a day of the week on which women can play for lower rates.

- Some public courses sell special annual, seasonal, or monthly memberships that enable golfers to play as often as they wish for free on weekdays and/or for free or steeply discounted rates on weekends. These can be very good deals for people who expect to play a lot at a particular course.

- In many areas, it is possible to purchase discount coupon books that enable you to play different courses in the region once or twice at sharply reduced rates (sometimes free) during the week, or that offer more modest discounts on weekends and after you have used up your initial visits. You can find these deals and others on the Internet or advertised in the newspaper or area golf magazine.

- Finally, in areas where there are a lot of golf courses, you can find services on the Internet and advertised in travel publications that will book last-minute tee times at discounted rates, subject to availability. These services are especially useful when you are traveling to resort areas and have flexibility with respect to where and when you can play.

Getting a Tee Time

Tee times may be reserved in advance at nearly all golf clubs by calling the pro shop. The person who answers the phone also will be glad to provide information about greens fees, including reduced rates for older golfers, twilight play, and any other specials the club may offer. He or she may inform you about the club's dress code (see below) and may ask for a credit card number to reserve your tee time. Increasingly, it is possible to reserve tee times for many courses on the Internet.

Walking On

Especially when golf courses are not crowded, any public course will do its best to accommodate walk-ons (golfers who arrive without a tee time). Obviously, it is easier to walk on as a single than as a group of two or three. Ordinarily, as a single player, you will be added to an existing twosome or threesome.

When You Arrive at the Course

Bag drop

Almost all golf courses have a place to drop off your golf bag close to the clubhouse before you park your car. Unless you are playing at a very upscale private club, most golfers change into their golf shoes before leaving their car in the parking lot. At more elegant clubs, you are expected to change in the locker rooms.

Tipping

Most private clubs, resort courses, and upscale public golf clubs employ young men (sadly, rarely women) whose job it is to assist golfers with their equipment upon arrival at the club and after completing their rounds. At some clubs (even though they may be open to the public), these services also may include cleaning and storage of clubs for members. If you are greeted by someone at the bag drop area who takes your clubs and puts them onto a golf cart, it is customary to tip them a dollar or two per bag. Another dollar or two per bag is appropriate after your round for the person who cleans your clubs. When you are playing at such a club, make sure that you have some available "dollars for the boys" in your wallet or golf bag.

Check-in

Before you pick up your clubs from the bag drop, check in at the pro shop to confirm your tee time, pay for your round, and rent a power cart unless you plan to walk. If you have time to warm up on the practice range, inquire whether your greens fees include practice balls and, if not, buy a token for the ball machine or purchase a small bucket of balls. Before you leave the counter, ask where you will find the starter and how you will be notified to move to the first tee.

The starter

The person in charge of making sure you get to the tee on time is the starter. He or she will check your receipt to make sure you have paid your fees, tell you how to get to the first tee, and give you instructions about the course, including the position of the pins on each hole and the cart path rules for the day. Many courses don't employ starters.

Etiquette on the Course

In addition to its formal rules, golf has a number of customs and informal rules that help to make it such a civilized game. Here are some of the most important.

Respect the course

A golf course is composed primarily of living plants, mainly grass. Continual smashing with steel and titanium clubs and the pounding caused by the fall of golf balls hit hundreds of feet into the air, not to mention golfers constantly walking on the grass and golf carts driving all over it, produce a lot of wear and tear. One of the first responsibilities of all golfers, therefore, is to do everything possible to protect and maintain the course. Each course has its own rules, which must be followed by all golfers. These include the following:

• Replace or replant divots. Many courses ask golfers to replace divots (chunks of grass and dirt torn up when you hit the ball); that is, pick up the divot and put it back into the hole it came from. Some courses provide golfers with bottles that contain a mixture of sand and grass seed, and golfers are asked them to pour the mixture into the holes they make.

• Repair ball marks (indentations caused by balls landing) on greens. There is a special tool for this purpose, but a golf tee also will work. One of the first things you will learn from your teaching professional is how to use a repair tool.

• Follow the rules for golf carts that are in effect when you play. When the course is dry, most courses will permit golf carts to drive on the course, except near greens (where signs will direct carts to the cart path). If there is no starter, signs are often posted to inform you at the beginning of your round of the rules governing carts on that day, including any holes where you are prohibited from driving on the course. Whatever the rules, use common sense when driving your cart on the course: For example, avoid wet areas to minimize wear and tear on the course.

• Always keep all carts, including pull carts, off greens.

• Rake bunkers after you have hit your ball out of them.

Respect other players

• Don't talk or move around while another player is hitting his or her ball. Stand directly facing and slightly behind players hitting from the tee so you can watch their ball and tell them where it went if they aren't able to follow its flight. Beginners and older golfers like me with less than perfect eyesight often have a hard time seeing where their ball lands. It's not good sportsmanship to make negative comments after a bad shot, but compliments and supportive remarks after a good shot are usually welcome.

• The player having the lowest score on the previous hole has the right to tee off first if he or she wishes (honors). Honors carry over if everyone has the same score on the next hole.

• After tee shots, the player farthest from the hole customarily plays his or her ball first. Both as a courtesy and in order to avoid being struck by a wayward shot, other players should stay behind the player who is hitting the ball. When playing *ready golf*—where whoever is ready first plays first—this courtesy is agreed to be dropped.

• Don't hit your ball until players in the group ahead of you are well out of your range. If you hit a ball sideways that could endanger players on an adjacent hole, warn them by calling out (loudly) "Fore." This means, "watch out, incoming ball."

On the green

• The flagstick should be left in the hole until all players' balls are on the green, and then removed before anyone putts. (Statistically, the flagstick gives players hitting from off the green a slightly greater chance of sinking their shot. Any player may request that the stick be removed at any time, however.) A player whose ball is on the green may ask another player to "tend" the flagstick—hold the stick upright in the hole until the putt is struck—but it must be removed before any putt goes into the hole to avoid a penalty. Gently lay the flagstick down out of the way of any possible putts.

• A player is permitted to mark the spot where his ball sits on the green and pick the ball up to clean it before making his putt. Players *must* put down a mark and remove their ball if their ball is close to the path of another player's putt, or at the request of any other player. If your mark is on or very close to the line of another player's putt, you should move your mark one or more putter-head distance on either side of the line at the other player's request. Be sure you have a coin or ball marker in your pocket before you begin your round. As with other shots, the player farthest from the hole putts first.

• In my experience, most recreational golfers concede putts within one or two feet of the hole. One of the other players says, "That's good," when your ball stops a foot from the hole, though *you still have to count the conceded putt.* However, every golf book I have ever read says you should get in the habit of making every putt if there will ever be an occasion on which you must sink them all (for example, in a tournament or competitive league play).

• While you are on the green, avoid stepping on the line of another player's putt at any time. Avoid moving around or talking while another player is putting.

Keep up the pace of play

The single most important piece of advice on etiquette for any new golfer is that you should learn to play quickly enough to maintain the pace of play. Many golf clubs provide players with a schedule of recommended times it takes to play each hole (on average, about fifteen minutes) and the club urges all golfers to maintain this pace. In my opinion, there are few things more annoying in the game of golf than being stuck behind a group of golfers who fall far behind this pace because they are spending too much time looking for balls hit into the rough or woods, too much time deliberating over their shots, or, worst of all, are simply not paying attention to the fact that they are taking too much time.

Of course, the more shots you take and the more balls you hit into the trees, the longer it is going to take you to play each hole. Moreover, many older golfers aren't able to move as quickly on the course as they once were. However, here are a number of things all golfers can and should do to help speed up play, particularly when the course is crowded.

- The major reason golfers fall behind the pace of play is because one or more of the members of the group has to search for a lost ball. It is one thing to watch your ball disappear into the woods or a lake and know (or be pretty sure) that it is gone. If this happens, hit another ball, take your penalty if you are keeping score, and move on. (If you aren't sure if the ball is lost, hit a provisional ball, then, if you can't find your first one, you can play your second shot and take the penalty.)

But what if you have hit what you thought was a decent shot and you can't find your ball? It may be hiding in the rough, or have taken a bad bounce, or you didn't notice exactly where it landed. One of the most aggravating experiences in golf is to have to give up on finding your ball, especially when you are having a good round. Bottom line, however: If you can't find your ball after several minutes, declare it lost and play another ball from that spot on the course (if you are playing according to strict rules, you must hit another ball from the spot of the previous shot unless you have hit a provisional ball).

- Help prevent lost balls by watching and concentrating on where balls hit by other members of your group land.
- Be ready to hit your shot when it's your turn. If you are riding in a cart and aren't sure what club you will use for your next shot, take several clubs with you to the ball so that you don't have to run back and forth to the golf cart for a different club. Do your shot planning and take your practice swings while other players are hitting their shots (provided

that you aren't interfering with another player's concentration). Don't forget to pick up your extra clubs after you hit your shot.

• Move reasonably quickly *between* shots so you don't have to cut short your preparation or pre-shot routines. Pay attention to the most efficient route to your and your golf cart partner's balls. Get on and off greens as quickly as possible. The more time you can save getting ready to hit your shots, the more relaxed you will be when it's your turn to swing a club.

Advice from the Pro
Play "Ready Golf"

When your course is crowded on a Saturday or Sunday morning and there is pressure on everyone to keep up the pace of play, play *ready golf.* This means that players who are ready to hit their next shot don't wait for their turn according to protocol, assuming that they can do so without interfering with or endangering other members of their group. It's proper etiquette to use honors on each tee (the person with the lowest score on the previous hole gets to hit first). Be ready when it's your turn to hit. —Mary Beth

• If your group is playing slowly and there is only one group behind you, invite the group behind to *play through,* which means to let them move ahead of your group on the course. This courtesy works if the hole ahead of your group is open and is particularly appropriate if there are only two or three players in the group behind. It doesn't help if there are several groups backed up ahead of or behind you.

• As a last resort, if the course is especially crowded and

your group is unable to maintain the pace of play, the course marshal may request that you split your foursome into two groups of two. Two twosomes can move faster than one foursome and this can help relieve the congestion on the course behind you. The course marshal also might ask your group to skip a hole in order to speed up play. If this happens, forget about your score and move on.

Advice from the Pro
Rule #1 for New Golfers—Play Quickly

As a teaching professional, I enjoy the experience of playing golf with new golfers. I understand that it takes new players more shots to get to the green. However, even I lose patience when new golfers take a lot of shots *and* are slow. If nine holes of golf take your groups much more than two hours (and you are not being held up by the group in front of you), you're playing too slowly. I understand how much information you think there is to remember and your "checklist of reminders" may seem endless. However, slow play is intolerable. If it takes you a long time to set up for each shot, you need to really walk or ride fast between shots to save time elsewhere. Do your thinking while others are hitting, so when it's your turn to hit, you're ready to go.

Selecting a course that isn't real busy or picking a time of day when there aren't a lot of people playing are good strategies for new players who wish to take extra time playing a round.

The amount of time it takes to play golf is often cited as the number-one reason people quit playing the game. Being a new golfer does not have to be synonymous with being a slow golfer. Do your part to speed up play and the game will be far more enjoyable for everyone. —Mary Beth

Backswings

- Don't try to play golf until you have spent some time on a practice range.
- You don't have to play eighteen holes.
- Choose less difficult courses in the beginning (or bring lots of extra golf balls).
- If possible, try to play when the course isn't crowded.
- Pay attention to the etiquette of golf.
- Maintain the pace of play.

Chapter 6

Playing by the Rules: When It's Important, When It's Not

*The secret to good golf is to hit the ball hard,
straight, and not too often.*

Golf is the only major sport in the world in which participants themselves enforce the rules. Most golf courses have marshals/rangers, whose primary responsibilities are to make sure that golfers maintain the pace of play, enforce local rules regarding power carts, and render assistance to players. Except in high-level tournament play, there is no referee. Golfers are simply expected to play by the rules. Because golfers are widely scattered during the course of play, you are often the only person who knows whether you are playing by the rules.

Most golfers know the major rules of the game and, remarkably, in my experience, most play by the rules, whether anyone else is paying attention or not. Within the rules of golf, however, there are several different, unofficial, "sets of rules" that are used by most recreational golfers much of the time. In tournament play and in competitive, serious golf, all players adhere strictly to the official rules of the United States Golf Association. In "social golf" or "business golf," the official rules are usually relaxed and significant modifications are adopted by the players themselves. For example, one or more "mulligans" (free do-over shots) might be permitted in the course of a round and short putts ("gimmies") often are conceded. The most common variations are discussed below, but let's start with the basics.

When it comes to the rules, there are two steps new golfers should follow:

- Become familiar with the basic rules of golf.
- Find out what variations are permitted in your group.

If you are playing by yourself, or keeping your own score as an independent member of a group, it is up to you to decide what modifications of the official rules you will allow yourself. In the beginning, as Mary Beth suggests in the accompanying box, you should be very lenient with yourself. As your game improves, you may decide to begin testing yourself against the more stringent rules of the USGA, or you and your regular playing partners may settle on a particular subset of rules that you are all comfortable with. If you decide to establish and maintain an official USGA handicap (see below), you will have to stick to the official rules.

Learn the Basics

Rule 1.1. The Game of Golf consists in playing a ball from the teeing ground into the hole by a *stroke or successive strokes* in accordance with the *Rules.*

Advice from the Pro
Use "New Golfer Rules"

In the early learning stages, I recommend to my students that they use specially designed "new golfer rules," which include such liberties as "do-overs" (when time allows) and teeing up all shots, including chips, pitches and all fairway shots. I also teach new golfers my "ten-second rule." If they whiff or top a shot, I tell them to re-hit another ball, and if they can do it within ten seconds, they don't have to count that miserable first shot. From my perspective, it's not cheating when you announce up front that you're a new golfer and your teacher encourages you to intentionally bend the rules somewhat to create a more positive playing experience.

No, these are not the real rules of the game, but my philosophy is to make sure that new golfers have fun. The game of golf is difficult enough as it is and I don't subscribe to the school of thought that says students need to suffer in order to learn a new skill. Giving yourself a few more opportunities to hit good shots will increase your confidence and keep you coming back to the course. —Mary Beth

Rule 13.1. The ball shall be played as it lies, except as otherwise provided in the *Rules.*

These two rules (as excerpted from *The Rules of Golf as approved by the United States Golf Association and The Royal and Ancient Golf Club of St. Andrews, Scotland)* are the basis for nearly all of the really important rules of golf. The first says that you have to keep hitting the ball (and, by implication, counting your strokes) until the ball is in the hole. The second says that you must play the ball as it lies, unless granted an exception under the rules. If you can't do either of these things—for example, because you lose your ball in the woods or are unable to hit it because it's underneath some bushes—the rules tell you what to do, including recording one or more penalty strokes. The official rules of golf cover all aspects of the game of golf, including the differences between match play and stroke play, the number of clubs you may carry, characteristics of golf balls, players' responsibilities while on the course, the order of play, other forms of play, and the administration of the rules themselves. For all golfers, however, the most important rules of golf concern things that happen to your golf ball during the course of play.

Lost balls, water hazards, and unplayable lies

All golf courses are designed to reward accuracy and penalize errant shots. Many things can happen to your golf ball when you make a poor shot, and some unexpected things happen even when you hit the ball well. If you were able to hit every ball perfectly from tee to green, keeping your ball in the fairway and avoiding every hazard, you would not have to worry about most of the rules of golf. You'd also be on the pro tour. The most frequently invoked rules of golf concern what happens when one of the following occurs:

- You can't find your ball (lost ball).
- You hit your ball out of bounds (off the course).
- You hit your ball into a hazard (water or bunker).
- You are unable to hit your ball for any one of several reasons, including natural or manmade obstructions (unplayable lie).

Lost ball

A ball is considered "lost" if it cannot be found within five minutes after you start looking for it. If it is lost, you must go back to the spot from which you last played and play another, counting both your first and second shots and adding a penalty stroke. If the lost ball was played from the tee, you are allowed to hit your next shot from a tee, but, in terms of stroke count, you are hitting your third shot.

This severe penalty is called "loss of stroke and distance," (LSD) meaning that if you lose your ball, you are penalized any distance you achieved on your first shot, plus a penalty stroke. Example: You hit your tee shot into the woods or long grass and can't find it after looking for it for the allotted five minutes. You must return to the tee and hit another, recording a total of three strokes so far. This penalty applies any time you can't find your ball, not just when you hit from the tee. Thus, if you can't find the ball after hitting your second shot, you must return to the place where you hit the second shot. After re-hitting your second shot, you will be "lying four." Lying four in this example includes strokes for your tee shot, your second shot (which was lost), a penalty stroke, and your re-hit, following the lost ball.

Exceptions: There are two main exceptions to the foregoing rule:

- If you are certain that your ball is lost in "ground under repair" (formally designated by local rules), or "casual water" (for example, rain water), or an animal hole, then you do not have to take a penalty stroke for a lost ball and may drop a new ball at the "nearest point of relief," for example, near where your ball entered the abnormal condition.
- If your ball is lost in a water hazard, or a locally designated "lateral hazard," a different rule applies (see Water Hazard, below).

Ball out-of-bounds
The penalty for hitting your ball out-of-bounds is the same as for a lost ball: that is, *stroke and distance.* The boundaries of the

course may be a fence, or they will be marked with white stakes or a white line on the ground.

Ball in water hazard

If your ball goes into a water hazard (lake, pond, river, drainage ditch, or other open water), you have the option of

---

Advice from the Pro
Play a Provisional Ball

If you think there is a chance your tee shot is lost (not in a water hazard) or has gone out-of-bounds, the rules permit you to hit a provisional shot in order to avoid having to go all the way back to the tee in the event that you can't find your first ball. You must inform your playing partners that you are hitting a provisional ball. If you can't find your first ball, or it has landed out-of-bounds, play your provisional ball, which is "lying three," including a one stroke penalty. If you find your original ball, you may pick up the provisional ball without penalty.
—Mary Beth

---

playing another ball from the spot where you hit into the hazard, counting both strokes and adding a penalty stroke (LSD). Or, you may drop a new ball anywhere behind the hazard on a line drawn from the hole through the spot where your first ball entered the hazard. If your ball lands in a lateral water hazard, you have the additional option of dropping a new ball within two club lengths of the spot where it entered the hazard, on either side of the hazard, but no closer to the hole. In each case, you must add a penalty stroke.

Sometimes creek beds dry out in drought conditions. If your ball is playable, you may play it without penalty, provided you do not ground your club. Grounding a club means touching the ground behind the ball or taking a practice swing during which you strike the ground or the grass. Environmentally sensitive areas from which golfers are prohibited are treated as water hazards. There is usually a sign designating these areas.

Unplayable lie

If your ball ends up under a bush, against, or behind, a tree or rock, or in some other spot (not in a water hazard) where it is difficult to hit, you must decide whether you wish to play it or not. If you decide to play it "as is," you must play it as it lies. If you determine that the ball is unplayable, you have three options:

- You may hit another shot from the place where you hit the previous shot, counting both strokes, plus a penalty stroke (LSD).
- Or, adding one penalty stroke, you may 1) drop a ball within two club lengths of the spot where the ball lay (but not nearer the hole) or 2) drop a ball any distance *behind* the spot where the ball lay on a line drawn from the flag through the spot where it lay. (If the original spot from which you made the errant shot was from a bunker, the place where you drop must also be in the bunker.)

There are several exceptions to the foregoing rules regarding unplayable lies. These exceptions specify the conditions when a golfer is entitled to obtain *relief* from a bad lie.

- *Artificial obstructions.* If your ball is near a moveable artificial obstruction, such as a distance marker, rake or a hose, you may move the obstruction. If a fixed artificial obstruction, such as a sprinkler head, maintenance shed, or a cart path, interferes with your swing or your stance, you may drop your ball without penalty within one club length of the nearest point of relief, but no closer to the hole.

• *Casual water, ground under repair, animal holes.* If your ball lies in or touches any of the foregoing, or if any of these things interfere with your stance or swing, you may pick up the ball and drop it within one club length of the nearest point of relief without penalty, but no closer to the hole, as long as your ball is not in a bunker. If it is in a bunker under any of these conditions, you may take the same degree of relief provided you do not remove the ball from the bunker. You are also permitted to drop the ball outside the bunker under these adverse conditions, although you may move the ball no closer to the hole, and you must take a one-stroke penalty.

Loose impediments

On many occasions you will find your ball amidst "loose impediments" (leaves, sticks, stones, or fallen branches) that impede your swing. This is especially likely in the fall, and on those occasions when you hit your ball into woods that line the course. You are permitted to remove any such loose material, so long as you don't cause your ball to move. You may not tear out plants or break branches to get a better shot. (However, you are allowed to hit and break plants in the course of your swing.)

Dropping your ball

The USGA Rules of Golf are very specific about the procedure for dropping a ball whenever this is called for under the rules. The rules require that the golfer stand erect, hold the ball at shoulder height and at arm's-length, and drop it straight downward. You may face any direction, but if the ball touches you or your equipment while falling, you must drop it again. You must also re-drop it if it rolls (a) into or out of a hazard, (b) onto a putting green, (c) out-of-bounds, (d) more than two club-lengths from where it first struck the ground, (e) back into the condition from which relief was taken, or (f) nearer to the hole.

A Few Other Things You Should Know

The preceding rules cover the most common things that can and will happen to your golf ball before you reach the green on each hole during a round of golf. Here are a few other rules you need to know. Whether you are scrupulous about observing them, or not, is up to you, although in competition play, they must be strictly observed.

Whiffing

If you swing at the ball with the intention of hitting it, it counts as a stroke whether you make contact with the ball or not. (However, if the ball accidentally falls off the tee you can replace it without penalty.) Unless there is money at stake, most golfers I play with don't happen to notice such embarrassing moments.

Moving your golf ball

If you accidentally cause your ball to move while you are getting ready to hit it, it counts as a stroke. This happens to everyone once in a while and you can decide whether your sense of honor compels you to record an extra stoke in your Sunday morning game with friends. If it's a tournament, you don't have a choice.

Playing the wrong ball

Playing the wrong ball costs you a two-stroke penalty unless the incorrect ball is in a hazard, in which case there is no penalty if you then play your own ball. (The latter exception is because the ball you play may be buried in the sand and you have no way of knowing whose it is without turning it over, which you aren't allowed to do.)

Grounding your club in a hazard

It is against the rules to ground your club in a hazard—that is, touch the sand or water with it—before making your downstroke. The penalty is two strokes.

On the Green

A special set of rules applies to players once they reach the putting green. The most important of these are the following:

Ball hitting the flagstick
If your ball hits the flagstick when you play from the putting green, whether the flagstick is in or out of the hole, you automatically lose the hole in match play and incur a two-stroke penalty in stroke play. If you are playing your ball from anywhere off the green and the ball hits the flagstick, there is no penalty.

Marking your ball's position on the green
If another player's ball lies on the line of your putt, you may request that it be lifted. The other player must mark its position with a coin or other flat marker immediately behind the ball. If the marker might interfere with your putt, it may be moved one or more putter-head-lengths away from the line of your putt. On the green, you are permitted to pick up and clean your ball, although you must mark its position.

Ball hitting another player's ball
In stroke play, if both balls are on the green and your ball hits another player's ball, you incur a two-stroke penalty. The ball you hit is returned to its original position and you must play your ball from where it lies. There is no penalty in match play.

Local Rules

Golf courses are permitted by the USGA to establish local rules pertaining to special features or conditions of the course, within parameters set by the USGA. In particular, local rules may designate certain areas of the course as "environmentally sensitive" (areas from which golfers are prohibited). Local rules may also deal with temporary conditions such as "ground under repair" and areas of mud, extreme wetness and generally poor conditions. Some courses establish "winter rules" that enable golfers, for example, to move their balls to grassy areas on the fairways during winter months or when the course is in especially poor condition. Even the pros are sometimes permitted to "lift, clean, and place" their balls when playing conditions are especially poor. Local rules also may establish clearly marked "drop areas" when balls are hit into water hazards.

There are some points of etiquette to follow here too:

• Never take your pull cart or your golf bag onto the green. (Obviously, don't drive your power cart anywhere near the green.)

• Don't allow the flagstick to dent the green when you remove it from the hole.

• Repair all marks made by golf balls that have landed on the green.

The Most Common Variations

As noted at the beginning of this chapter, the majority of recreational golfers incorporate a few variations from the official rules of golf into the game. As discussed previously and below, almost universal outside the world of really serious golf is the acceptance of "gimmies" and "mulligans." In addition, as you play the game more frequently, you can expect to see a few other common departures from the rules.

Gimmies

A "gimmie" is a short putt that is conceded by your playing partners. You still must count the stroke, but you don't have to actually make the putt. The criteria for what counts as a "gimmie" (that is, how close to the hole your ball must be) can vary. Often, one of the players simply says "That's good" and you pick up your ball. A commonly used and less subjective standard is whether the ball's distance from the hole is less than the distance from the head of your putter to the leather handle. One group of friends that I play with uses this standard unless the putt is for par or birdie, in which case it must be holed. A phenomenon that I have frequently observed is the concession of longer and longer putts when a player is having a particularly bad day. In any case, as it is so often in golf, it's up to the players.

Mulligans

A mulligan is a free do-over: an opportunity to re-hit a shot without counting the first shot or recording a penalty stroke. Obviously, this is a clear violation of the "real" rules of golf, but, as any golfer will tell you, it sure makes you feel better to know that you can "take a mulligan" when you top your ball or hit it into a pond or deep into the woods. There are endless variations on the use of mulligans.

- At one extreme, if you are playing with either good friends or tolerant strangers (and not for money), you can award yourself a mulligan after any shot you take, so long as it doesn't slow the play of your group too much. After all, it's your score that you are keeping. After the round, you can say: "I broke 100, not counting the three mulligans I took."

- Many groups informally establish a policy about mulligans at the beginning of the round. A common practice is to allow each player a mulligan on the first tee, especially when you have arrived late and haven't had time to warm up (Mary Beth calls this "a breakfast ball"). A specific number of mulligans might be permitted during the course of the round, to be taken at each player's discretion. In this case, deciding when to take your available mulligan(s) becomes part of the strategy of the game.

- Many tournaments (especially charity events) and

golf leagues formally incorporate mulligans as a way of adding to the enjoyment of the competition. Charity golf tournaments often permit golfers to "purchase" mulligans before the round as a way of raising more money and adding to the excitement. Regular men's and women's golf leagues often specify a different format each week, on some occasions allowing each participant one or more mulligans in the course of his or her round.

Other Common Modifications to the Rules

New golfers may lose four or five balls in the course of an eighteen-hole round of golf. These include balls hit into water hazards, long grass or woods, as well as balls that didn't appear to be badly hit, but simply can't be found in the allotted five minutes. In addition to lost balls, there are likely to be some balls hit out-of-bounds and several unplayable lies in the same round.

As noted above, the official rules of golf impose strict penalties in all such situations, including, in addition to extra strokes, returning to the place where you hit your previous shot if you can't find your ball, and imposing limits on what you can do with your ball even if you are able to find it in the woods. Even if one is conscientious about hitting provisional balls, careful observance of the rules takes time that most foursomes don't have on a Sunday afternoon on a crowded golf course. In my experience, most recreational golfers are accustomed to simply recording a penalty stroke in all such situations and either moving their ball to a place where they can hit it or dropping a new ball. The complexity of the rules associated with balls lost or out-of-bounds, or balls that land in unplayable lies is thereby reduced, to the following simple phrase used to figure out how many strokes you have taken: "One [shot] in [the pond, woods, grass, etc.]; one out [ball moved out or new ball dropped]; hitting three." Yes, in most cases this isn't quite according to the rules, but, as an exasperated member of my foursome said to me while I was trying to figure out what to do after I hit my fourth consecutive ball into the woods: "What do you think this is, the PGA championship? Pick it up and drop it in the rough next to the fairway. Let's go."

Establishing a Handicap

Most competitive golf requires every player to have a handicap. This can include the Sunday morning foursome with your friends who like to play one or more of golf's competitive games with a few dollars at stake. Handicaps make it possible for golfers of different skill levels to compete on an equal basis. In general, handicaps reflect the difference between your average score for eighteen holes and par at most golf courses. A twenty-eight handicap means that your *average* score on *most* courses is 100 (par 72 + 28 additional strokes during your average round = 100). Here's how the system works.

When you decide to establish an official handicap, you must begin to keep accurate hole-by-hole scores for every round or partial round of golf you play (not counting practice rounds), in accordance with all applicable USGA rules. If you belong to a golf club or play regularly at a course that offers this service, you enter your scores on a computer (usually located in the pro shop), along with information about the course you played and the number of holes you played (usually nine or eighteen). If you don't belong to a club, you can establish a handicap online at a site such as golfserve.com (there is a modest membership fee, and you must agree to follow all of the rules and report your scores truthfully).

The system calculates the difference between your scores and the official course rating from the tees you played (black, white, blue, or red, usually). It then adjusts the result to take into account the course's difficulty, based on its slope rating. For example, if your total score is ninety on a course that has a course rating of sixty-eight and a slope rating of 113 (average), the contribution to your handicap average would be twenty-two.

In order to make sure that one or two particularly bad holes don't unduly influence your handicap, there is a limit on the score you can enter for any one hole, once again based on your handicap. This is called *Equitable Stroke Control*. It can be as low as double-bogey on any given hole; it is never more than nine strokes on any hole.

After you have entered scores for a minimum of five eighteen-hole rounds (nine-hole scores are combined), the system recalculates your handicap each time you enter a new score, eventually always taking the average of the ten best of your most recent twenty rounds.

How Handicaps Work

In stroke competition—which is based on the total number of strokes you take for nine or eighteen holes—your net score is the total number of strokes, minus your handicap.

In match play—which is based on the number of individual holes you or your team wins—you are allowed zero, one, or two strokes on each hole based on your handicap. If your handicap is eighteen or less, you get one stroke per hole, in order, beginning with the most difficult hole on the course. (That's why each hole is rated for difficulty on your scorecard.) If your handicap is over eighteen, you get one stroke for every hole and two strokes for the most difficult holes until all of your handicap strokes have been used up.

Example: A scratch golfer (zero handicap) and a nine-handicap player (Team A) are competing against an eighteen-handicap and a nine-handicap golfer (Team B) in match play. Team A gets a stroke off on each of the nine hardest holes on the course. Team B gets two strokes on the same nine most difficult holes and one stroke on each of the other nine holes. The team with the lowest number of total strokes, after handicap strokes are subtracted, wins the hole; if both teams have the same score, the hole is scored as a tie (AS, for "all square").

Giving Strokes

It is not necessary to establish a formal handicap to "give strokes" to people you are playing with and against. For example, my wife and I often play with another couple on Saturday mornings. The "boys" often play against the "girls," with the girls being given one stroke per hole. To win a hole, the men must have a combined stroke total that is at least two strokes lower than the women's score.

Backswing

Learning the rules is part of learning how to play golf. And, the rules are an important part of the game. At the same time, it is important to understand that the rules are meant to ensure that everyone can enjoy the game, not to prevent people from playing. The best thing about golf is that it can be played and enjoyed by people who play the game for different reasons. If your goal is to establish a handicap and play the game seriously, you can be sure that you will be competing on a level playing field (even though it looks like a golf course) regardless of your skill level. If your goal is to have fun, get exercise, and enjoy the social aspects of the game, the rules can accommodate this, too.

Chapter 7

Course Management—A Must for Golfers over 50

A golf ball will always travel farthest when hit in the wrong direction.

A friend of mine who played tennis every day until he passed away at age 87 had a sign over his home tennis court that read: *"Age and treachery will defeat youth and strength every day."* The sport of golf doesn't encourage treachery, but the principle that intelligence and strategy can help compensate for differences in physical capabilities is certainly applicable to golf, particularly when it comes to people over 50. Most tour professionals can hit *each one of their clubs,* on average, seventy-five to 100 yards farther than I can. If one takes pure distance out of the equation, however, everyone faces the same challenges on the course; namely, to hit shots that *are within our range* consistently and accurately. My first (and only) eagle came on a ninety-yard shot that went into the hole. I have sunk several forty-foot putts, just like the pros do on Sunday afternoon. So I know I *can* make such shots. I just don't do it very often. Unlike most racquet sports, golf doesn't require players to return shots hit by an opponent who is much better, stronger, and faster. The only true opponents in golf are yourself and the golf course.

Course management simply means figuring the best strategy to minimize risks and maximize your chances of getting your ball into the hole with the fewest number of strokes. Another way of looking at it is to determine the things you can do to achieve the greatest rewards and have the most fun on the course. And, what you do off the course—for example in practice—can increase your choices and improve your decisions when you get to the course.

Let's begin with one of the most important decisions you make each time you play golf, one that you must make before you hit your first shot: What tees are you going to play from?

The First Principle: Play from the Tees that Fit Your Game

The purpose of having different sets of tees is to reduce the advantage that sheer ability to hit the ball a long way gives (mostly) younger, stronger players. Shorter distances give beginners, older male players, and women a better chance to score as well as stronger players, assuming they can hit the ball with accuracy and consistency. I have alternated back and forth between the "normal" white tees and the forward, usually gold, tees since I began playing golf, often succumbing to peer pressure of my playing partners to play from the longer white tees. When the other three members of your foursome say: "Let's play from the white tees" it is very difficult for most men, even older novices like me, to say: "Go ahead, but I prefer to play from the forward tees."

A growing number of courses now offer suggestions about which tees golfers should play, based on their skill levels. For example, the back tees usually are recommended for men with handicaps under ten, the white tees for handicaps between ten and twenty-four, and the forward tees for men with handicaps twenty-five and up. Beginners, of course, usually don't have handicaps, but if your average score is over 100 for eighteen holes, you can assume that your handicap is over twenty-five. Thus, I strongly recommend that any man taking up the game for first time over the age of 50 play from the forward tees, at least until you are breaking 100 regularly. Most women should play from the red (most forward) tees.

The more you improve, the more you can appreciate the forward tees.

Despite occasional pressures from my playing partners to play from the longer tees, I have concluded that I have more fun playing from the forward tees. Curiously, this conclusion has been prompted by *improvements* in the level of my game. As the consistency of my game has slowly increased, so has the frequency with

Twenty-five Yards Makes a Big Difference

On most courses, the total distance from the gold or forward tees ranges from 300 to 600 yards less than the distance from the regular (white) tees, an average of between fifteen and forty yards per hole. This doesn't sound like much, but for older golfers this can make a big difference. Many older players still hit the ball with accuracy, but everyone loses distance as they age. My best tee shots travel an average of less than 175 yards. From the fairway, I can't count on hitting my second shot much farther than 150 yards, at most. On a 350-yard par four hole—a typical distance from the white tees—I have no hope of reaching the green in "regulation" (two shots), no matter how accurate my shots. On a 325-yard hole, I have a much better chance to get close to the green after two shots, significantly increasing the possibility of making a par.

which I have found myself in a position to make an occasional par during a round of golf. For me, making par is a pretty big thrill. It makes me feel like I can actually play the game of golf.

Now, each time I make par (or the even rarer birdie), I look forward to doing it again. Even more important than making par is the feeling that I have a realistic chance to make par on most holes. Bottom line: I try to play from the forward tees whenever I can.

A Suggestion for Course Designers and Managers

The trend in golf course construction in recent years has been to make courses longer and longer ("more challenging"), in part to keep up with improvements in the technology used to make both clubs and balls, and in part because PGA Tour professionals, like all professional athletes, are getting better and stronger. This may make sense for expert players, but it offers few benefits for the average golfer. Despite improvements in technology, scores of average golfers have not improved in the last several decades. On the other hand, increasing the length and difficulty of golf courses runs the risk of discouraging new players, especially older men and women, during a period when everyone hopes for and expects a significant influx of new golfers.

Advice from the Pro
What about Tees for Older Women (and Juniors)?

Many of my older women students hit their best drives only 75 yards. It's my belief that such women have been neglected by the golf industry. Why don't more courses have a set of tees that measure a total of 3,800–4,200 yards? Call these tees whatever you like, but they will appeal to older women, kids, and even the super senior guys. —Mary Beth

Choosing the Right Club for Each Shot

After you have decided what set of tees to play from, the next important decisions you have to make concern which club to use for each of your shots as you progress from tee to green. In the beginning, it will seem to you as though all of your shots travel the same distance, no matter which club you use. As your swing improves and you experiment with the various clubs in your bag, however, you will begin to notice differences. You will discover that you can hit the ball farther with the longer clubs, but that it is more difficult to hit the ball consistently with them than it is with the shorter clubs. You will also begin to develop favorites among your clubs; that is, clubs with which you have greater confidence in your ability to hit the ball well than others. (Over time, you will find that even your favorite clubs sometimes let you down; like some friends, they can be fickle. And, you find that your favorites change.)

Advice from the Pro
Get to Know Your Clubs

Except for the putter, golf clubs differ from each other primarily in two ways: their length and the angle of the face with which they strike the ball. The longer the club, the more leverage you have when you swing at the ball and therefore the faster the clubhead is traveling when it strikes the ball. The angle of the face (loft) determines the ball's trajectory after it leaves your club. The longer (low-number) clubs have slightly angled faces designed to hit the ball farther with lower trajectories. Shorter (higher-number) clubs have faces with progressively greater angles designed to hit the ball higher into the air and for shorter distances. —Mary Beth

When you have been practicing and playing for a few months, you will begin to have some idea how far you can hit the ball with each of your clubs. This knowledge is the basis for the decisions you make on the course about which club to pull out of the bag for each shot and how hard you decide to swing at the ball.

Following a serious amount of practice and calculations on the driving range, coupled with experience on the course, the following are my best estimates of the distance I can hit each of my clubs with a full swing:

Pitching wedge	80–90 yards
9-iron	90–100 yards
8-iron	100–110 yards
7-iron	110–120 yards
6-iron	120–130 yards
5-iron	130–140 yards
4-hybrid	140–150 yards
11-wood	150–160 yards
7-wood	160–170 yards
Driver	170–180 yards

These are average maximum distances, assuming I hit the ball cleanly and include an allowance for some roll after the ball lands. However, they don't take into account the specific conditions that one encounters regularly on the course. Everyone must adjust his or her estimate of how far the ball will actually travel on each shot depending on answers to the following questions:

How far will my ball roll after it lands? Balls hit with a low trajectory are more likely to roll for some distance after they land, especially if the course is dry, the ground is firm and level, and your ball lands on the fairway or the green. Next time you are watching a golf tournament on television, notice how far most of the pros' drives bounce and roll along the fairway. On many of their drives, they are getting an extra fifty yards, or more, because of the roll. In contrast, if the course is wet, or if the shot lands on a steep uphill slope, you can't expect much roll. If the ball lands in the rough, all bets are off. The higher the trajectory of the shot, the less roll you should expect, unless the ball lands on a downhill slope.

Estimating how far your ball is likely to roll is critical for club selection, particularly when the total distance of your shot matters a lot; for example, when you are hitting to the green or playing a short shot to avoid a hazard (laying up). If there are no bunkers or other hazards between you and the green, you may plan to land a low trajectory shot short of the green, anticipating that the ball will roll onto the green. If you are close enough to the green, but there are hazards between you and the green, you will often use a high lofted club to try to land the ball on the green near the flagstick, hoping that it will stop quickly and not roll off the green.

Is my target uphill or downhill? The general rule of thumb in golf is that when your target is significantly above where you are standing you should use one or two "more clubs" (that is, clubs that you can hit farther) than you would otherwise need. The greater the elevation of the target, the more extra club distance you need to reach it. Conversely, when your target is downhill, you should use "less club." As your experience grows, your judgment about how much of an adjustment to make for elevation will improve. This is also an area where familiarity with a particular golf course helps a lot.

Can I hit the ball cleanly, or do I have a bad lie? My calculations of how far I can hit the ball with each of my clubs are based on the assumption that I can and will hit the ball cleanly. In fact, I don't always hit the ball cleanly and I know that hitting out of long grass significantly decreases my chances of getting good contact with the ball. Therefore, when my ball is in the rough (it often is), I also "take an extra club." (One of the differences between tour professionals and ordinary mortals such as you and me is the extraordinary wrist and forearm strength that is required to hit balls out of heavy rough.)

Hitting it "Pure"

One day I was playing with three men whom I met for the first time on the first tee. One of them was a much better golfer than the rest of us and after I hit a particularly good shot, he turned to me and said: "You hit that *pure*." Indeed, the sensation I felt when I hit the ball can best be described by the word "pure"—the club had struck the ball squarely in the center of its sweet spot without hitting the ground or, as far as I could tell, any grass. The collision of the club with the ball caused no shock or vibration in my hands or arms and even the sound was a muted "click." The flight of the ball was long and high and straight at the target. There was no doubt in my mind that I had hit the ball about as well as I was capable of hitting it with that particular club. "Puring it" on every shot is every golfer's dream.

Knowing where you are on each hole

Making the right decision about what club to hit requires, of course, that you have some idea where you are on each hole on the golf course. Most golf courses have markers on the course that denote 100 yards, 150 yards, 200 yards, and 250 yards to the center of the green. These markers usually include lines on the cart path and colored discs or stakes in the center of the fairway (red, white, blue and yellow, from nearest to farthest from the hole). Many courses also have exact distances to the center of the green printed on sprinkler heads located between the major distance markers.

Knowing the distance to the green is, of course, important. Equally important is figuring out the distance to hazards that lie between you and the green. Hitting your ball into a bunker or creek that turns out to be closer than you thought is very disappointing, to say the least.

Many courses sell yardage books that contain detailed information about distances between many locations, including hazards, on each hole. Golf carts at some upscale clubs provide exact GPS location and distance information on screens in the cart. Some golfers carry handheld range finders.

It is always worth checking your own visual estimates of distance if you can. There is no rule against asking your playing partners for help, especially if one of them has experience on the course. And, the more you play, the better you will become at estimating distances accurately.

Balancing risk and reward—
the advantages of "laying up"

Almost every shot involves some calculation of risk and potential reward. Most golfers, myself included, turn out to be unrequited gamblers on the golf course. My chances of reaching a green surrounded by bunkers 170 yards away with one shot are negligible. Nevertheless, I can rarely resist pulling my 7-wood out of my bag, hoping that, if I hit it perfectly, the ball will roll through the small gap I can barely see between bunkers and onto the green. Like the gambler at the slot machine, I don't win this bet very often, but once in a while I make it, which keeps me coming back for more.

If my bunker play were better, I might get away with this strategic decision, but it turns out that these gambles account for many of the sevens and eights on my scorecard. The risks include not only missing the first shot, but, more important, leaving yourself with another even more difficult shot, for example, from a bunker or deep rough.

Deliberately hitting a shorter shot to avoid a potential hazard or to increase the chances that your ball will end up in a good position to reach the green with your next shot is called "laying up." For many golfers, it is synonymous with "giving up." However, for older players, you should think of it as "the winning play."

The 3 S's: Shorter, Straighter, and Safer

If the score doesn't matter to you, it may be worth going for the green, no matter how risky the shot, because it is exciting on those rare occasions when you succeed. If score matters, then try to remember that shorter, straighter and safer is almost always better than longer and riskier. That is why my 81-year old father-in-law often breaks ninety for eighteen holes while rarely hitting any shot longer than 150 yards. Perhaps by the time I'm 81, I will have learned this lesson.

Trust Your Swing and Your Club

Another of the most irresistible mistakes novice golfers make is failing to trust their swing or their club (or both). If you are like me, I predict that you will have the following experience many times, as I have. I am standing in the center of the fairway, 100 yards from the flagstick, which is in the center of the green. I *know* that for me the correct choice of club is my 9-iron, but the flagstick looks so far away and I am afraid that I won't hit the ball cleanly. So, I pull my 8-iron out of the bag. One of two things then happens: (a) I ease up on my swing because in the back of my mind I am afraid of hitting the ball too far, with the result that I miss the shot entirely, or (b) I hit the ball cleanly, over the green.

You won't always hit the ball perfectly and you won't always make the correct club selection. But the best advice anyone can give is to trust both your swing and the club to deliver the shot you plan and hope for. Now, if I could only follow my own advice.

Don't swing harder with longer clubs

I often find myself trying to hit the ball harder with my longer clubs. The farther I am from my target, the harder my subconscious tells me I need to hit the ball, even though I know that the extra distance is primarily the club's responsibility, not mine. This also occurs when I am trying to make sure I hit the ball over a hazard, such as a lake or a tree. Bad things almost always happen when I try to swing harder. I tense up, my brain tells me to take a longer backswing to build up more power, and I start my swing before my body begins its rotation. When this happens, the chances are that I either top the ball or hit the ground with the club before striking the ball (this is called "chunking" the shot). Needless to say, either mistake produces exactly the opposite of the extra distance I thought I needed.

The driver

In his famous *Little Red Book of Golf*, Harvey Pennick says that no golfer should try to hit a driver until he or she can land nine out of ten consecutive 3-wood shots in the fairway. The driver is the longest club in the golf bag and, without doubt, the most difficult to hit consistently. The loft of most drivers is between nine and twelve degrees, which means that one has to hit the ball perfectly to get it into the air. Golf club manufacturers have increased the size of the clubhead and regularly promise in their advertisements that their clubs have a "larger sweet spot," "will enable you to hit the ball straighter and farther," and "are more forgiving of mistakes."

These new drivers *look* like they will enable you to hit the ball a mile and, besides, how could you miss with something that big and made of titanium to boot? Since we older players are always looking for something that will help us both hit the ball farther and automatically correct our mistakes, there is a lot of temptation to spend $400 for a new driver.

I did not carry a driver in my bag until I had been playing golf for three years. The driver I finally bought has a very flexible shaft and a loft of thirteen degrees (I had to look hard to find a driver with that much loft). I practiced with it on the driving range for nearly a year before I hit a ball on the course with it. And, I am still not sure that the feeling of exhilaration and extra few yards that accompany the occasional perfect shot are worth the penalty shots and bad lies it also contributes to my game.

If you feel you must play with a driver, practice with it a lot before you take it onto the course and don't be too disappointed when you don't hit the ball as far as you expect every time.

The Short Game

To this point, the discussion of strategic choices one makes on the course has been based on the assumption that all shots are taken with a full swing. As soon as you are closer to the green than the full-swing range of your shortest club (for me, roughly seventy-five yards) you can no longer take a full swing at the ball without hitting it too far. This means taking less than a full swing, which opens up a new range of choices. Now things get more complicated because, in addition to club choice, you have to consider how hard to hit the ball, how to hold the club, and what to do with your wrists and hands. This is called *the short game,* and it is the great equalizer among players because it requires different skills and different strategic decisions.

Setting aside the driver and the putter, there are basically four different things you can do with *any* of the other clubs in your bag that will change the distance, trajectory, and spin of the ball when you hit it.

- Change the amount of backswing—the shorter the backswing, the shorter the shot.
- Grip down on the club (shorten the length of the club by holding it down closer to the head and farther away from the end).
- Vary the amount of wrist, hand, and body action.
- Change the tempo of the swing.
- Vary the angle of the downswing.

Multiplying these adjustments to your swing by the number of clubs in your bag produces a bewildering array of possible combinations. If you have ever watched a golf tournament on television, you may have heard one of the commentators remark that a particular shot required great imagination on the part of the golfer. This comment is a testament to the creativity that is possible when considering how to make the best use of your clubs, particularly in the short game. Also, I should mention, this is one of the factors that makes golf such an entertaining—and challenging—game.

Advice from the Pro
Vary the Backswing

While each of the clubs in your bag has a primary function, most can also be used for other purposes by changing the way you swing. Let's take the 7-iron as an example. The 7-iron is used with a full swing to hit a relatively high lofted shot onto the green. It can also be used effectively with a short swing for a low, running chip from any position around the green. And, it can be used with a half-swing (waist-high backswing) to hit a shot from under a tree limb to get the ball back into the fairway. I teach my students that 80 percent of all distances in the short game can be achieved simply by changing the length of the backswing. s—Mary Beth

Chipping and pitching

In theory, most of the clubs in your bag can be used for shots inside seventy-five yards. Neither you nor I, however, have the luxury of thirty years playing golf to gain experience with the full range of possibilities that are available. So far, I have found that I rely on three clubs for the vast majority of shots that I hit near the green: the 7-iron, pitching wedge, and sand wedge. The two variables that determine my choice among these clubs are (a) how far I am from the hole, and (b) how much loft I need on the shot, either to clear an obstacle (a bunker, thick grass) or to help stop the ball when it lands on the green.

> ## Advice from the Pro
> ### Get the Ball Down and Rolling
>
> The general rule of thumb that applies to short shots to the green is that it is desirable to get the ball down on the ground and rolling as quickly as possible. If you are within a few yards of the green, you should chip with a lower lofted club like the 7-iron, one that gives you only enough height and distance to get the ball onto the green and rolling toward the hole. Shorten up on the club (move your hands down the handle) for greater control and vary the distance of your shot by adjusting the length of your backswing. — Mary Beth

If there is a bunker, or more than five to ten yards of rough, between you and the green, you will need a club that gives you enough loft—that is, a pitching wedge, sand wedge, or lob wedge—to carry the ball over this obstacle. The lower the trajectory of your shot, in general, the farther the ball will roll after it lands. The higher the trajectory, the shorter the roll will be. (Experts know how to control the spin on the ball in order to slow it down or allow it to "release" toward the hole after it lands on the green. I haven't learned how to do this yet, as it is a precise skill, learned only after years of practice.)

Bunker play

Speaking of bunkers, the first rule of course management is to do your best to stay out of them. Experienced golfers know how to hit the ball out of bunkers, and professionals are often relieved when their ball lands in the sand instead of deep grass or a water hazard. Until you have spent some serious time practicing hitting the ball out of the sand, however, I predict that this will be your least favorite part of the game. Every golf instruction book contains a section on bunker play, but there is no substitute for professional instruction and lots of practice.

Practicing to get "up and down"

Even playing from the forward tees, I rarely reach the green with my second shot on par 4s or my third shot on par 5s. And, I often miss the green on my tee shots on par 3 holes. As a result, I find myself pitching or chipping the ball to the green on the majority of holes I play. It is a safe bet to assume that you will, too. It is important to remember that the goal of all such shots is to get the ball close enough to the hole to give yourself a reasonable chance of getting the ball into the hole with one putt. This is called *getting up* (onto the green) and down (into the hole). Even more important than putting, therefore, is learning to chip and pitch the ball accurately to the hole from anywhere around the green. After all, three-foot putts are much easier to make than twenty-five-foot putts. As the credit card commercial might put it: "Not having to putt, *priceless.*"

When I am chipping and pitching well, my score improves dramatically. When I'm not, I've probably stopped keeping score.

The Importance of the Short Game

I had been playing for three and a half years when a friend invited me to be his playing partner in the member-guest tournament at a local military base golf club. My short game had improved, but I was still not breaking 100 with any consistency on real courses, and I accepted his invitation with considerable trepidation. In addition to two 18-hole rounds of golf (using four different formats), there was also to be a skills challenge on the evening before the tournament. In the skills challenge, each golfer was given two shots at each of seven different venues: a drive, a 100-yard shot, a thirty-yard pitch, a twenty-yard chip, a fifteen-yard shot through a hole in piece of plywood, a bunker shot, and thirty-foot putt. Each shot was scored for accuracy and when I landed my second 100-yard, 9-iron shot a few yards from the flagstick, I realized that all of my practice might not be for naught. I ended up scoring points on five of the seven skills and winning third place overall in the competition. Not surprisingly, I failed to score with my drives and my bunker shots.

For golfers over 50, the importance of the short game cannot be overemphasized.

There is really only one way to get better at making these shots and that is to practice them. Curiously, most golfers (no matter how old they are) don't spend much time practicing their short game. Few golfers on the driving range are hitting the ball with wedges, and it is more difficult to find practice areas that encourage (or even permit) chipping onto a green from a variety of different lies. One reason for this is that such shots can endanger golfers who are practicing putting on the green. Another is that longer chips and pitches will leave ball marks on the green.

It is worthwhile, therefore, to search out practice facilities nearby where you can practice all of the elements of the short game: pitching, chipping, and bunker play. Pitching and chipping can also be practiced in any modest-sized open area, including your backyard.

Backswings

- Play from the tees that fit your skills.
- Get to know your clubs.
- Know where you are on each hole.
- Balance risks and potential rewards of each shot.
- Leave your driver in your bag until you can hit the ball with it consistency.
- Practice your short game.

Chapter 8

Managing the Ups and Downs

"The same could not be said for first-round co-leader Davis Love III, who had his own nightmarish breakdown on this cool, breezy afternoon. A first-round co-leader after shooting 65 on Thursday, Love, the 1992 and 2003 champion, came in at 11-over-par 83 Friday, a bizarre 18-stroke swing from one of the finest players in the world, and missed the cut of even par 144 by four shots.

Starting on the back nine, Love double bogeyed the 14th hole, had six more bogeys and made quadruple bogey nine on his final hole, the 587 yard par 5 number 9, tying the highest number ever posted on that hole in this tournament on his way to his worst score in 21 appearances.

'Just one of those days,' Love said. 'I hit four or five drives that were bad, but then they went in really bad places. Sometimes I couldn't even chip out. I didn't hit enough good tee shots to give myself a chance to scramble. When I hit a bad shot, I never got away with it.'"

—*Washington Post*, March 3, 2006

A couple of years after I started playing golf, I called Mary Beth one evening and said: "I think I've finally got it." I had been playing pretty well for a couple of weeks and finally was beginning to feel more confident about my swing. Her response was: "You *never* get it; you just *borrow* it."

Golf is a game of ups and downs, perhaps more so than any other sport. Even the pros suffer from inconsistency in their play from day to day and week to week, and no one is exempt from an occasional truly ugly shot that prompts the question: "Where did that come from?" For most golfers, but especially for beginners, major fluctuations in the level of one's performance are a normal part of the game.

What's Different about Golf?

All athletes have good days and bad days, good shots and bad shots. So, what's different about golf that causes such extreme variations not only in performance (shot to shot, day to day), but also in one's score, particularly for beginners?

- *The complexity of the swing.* A good golf swing requires perfect synchronization of many different muscle groups, and a tiny variation in the path or angle of the clubhead at impact can have a huge impact on the flight of the ball. Thus, small mistakes are magnified, and it is often difficult to figure out what went wrong and how to correct the mistake.
- *Conditions vary.* After the tee shot, every shot on the golf course is different, often *very* different, from any shot you have taken before. The more golf you have played, the more experience you acquire hitting balls under widely varying conditions. Even experienced golfers, however, often encounter situations they have literally never seen before. It is easy to misjudge how hard you need to hit a ball lying in thick grass, how far the ball will roll after it lands, or whether you can avoid hitting a tree that stands between you and the green.

- *Every shot counts.* Every shot counts in a round of golf, whether it is a 200-yard drive or a two-foot putt. A bad shot, moreover, often makes the next shot more difficult. The eight you carded on the second hole is still there when you add up your score. However, a professional baseball player who only gets a hit once in every three times at bat is headed for the Hall of Fame.

- *Chance plays a bigger role.* Because of the widely varying characteristics of each hole on each golf course, luck comes into play more often than it does in other sports. On some days, balls that hit trees always seem to bounce into the woods; on other days, they bounce back out onto the fairway. Over time, of course, good and bad luck balance each other, but that knowledge doesn't do anything to reduce your anguish after a seemingly perfect shot takes a bad bounce off a sprinkler head and ends up in an unplayable lie.

For all of these reasons, golf can be an especially aggravating game. Since so much is riding on every shot, and there are so many things that can go wrong on each shot, *no golfer,* no matter how skilled, is immune from emotions that accompany each mistake or bad break. For beginners, mistakes are a constant part of the game. The more seriously you take the game, and the harder you try, the more likely you are to have to deal with these emotions on a regular basis. As a general rule, stress does not enhance any athletic performance, and golf is particularly vulnerable to its effects. Learning to manage these natural reactions, therefore, is an important part of the game of golf, not only for the benefit of your game, but also for the benefit of your playing partners.

Coping with the Downs

So, how do you cope with the ups and, especially, the downs of golf? The following are some suggestions that may prove helpful:

- *Focus on the ups, not the downs.* Even the rankest beginner makes a good shot now and then. Good shots may

Don't Throw Your Club

Each person reacts differently to adversity. Some people are by nature more volatile than others in their response to frustration and disappointment. The history of golf is replete with stories of players who were famous for throwing their clubs or otherwise violently expressing their reactions to a poor shot or bad break. Throwing one's club is a definite no-no in the book of golf etiquette.

be few and far between, but that only makes them more memorable. Keep track of them and remember what they felt like. You will *always* have some good shots to tell your friends about. In my group, we keep track of TOBs (*Things of Beauty*).

• *Keep your expectations under control.* It's okay to look forward to each new outing with optimism and the positive expectation that your score will be better than it was yesterday. However, it is very unlikely that you will suddenly play par golf when you have never broken 100. Statistically, the odds are that if you scored well yesterday, today will be worse, and vice versa. Modest expectations can help to minimize frustration and disappointment.

• *Don't let the first few holes get you down (or too far up).* A round of golf consists of nine or 18 holes. Try not to let your scores on the first couple of holes have a disproportionate effect on your emotions or expectations for the day. Scores usually balance out; if you are off to a good

When Your Game Improves, Watch Out

The better your game, the higher your expectations become and the greater the potential for disappointment and aggravation when you do make a mistake. In the early stages, poor shots are commonplace and are more likely to be taken in stride. Early on, I was happy when I only lost a few balls during the round and came close to breaking 100. As I improved, both my aspirations and expectations increased accordingly. Now, I am really annoyed by missed short putts that prevent me from having a really good round.

start, you are ahead of the game. If you have trouble at the beginning, things will almost certainly get better.

• *Play your round in three parts.* To lend yourself psychological balance, divide eighteen holes into three six-hole games; nine holes into three three-hole games.

• *Set attainable goals when you start playing golf.* Don't set unrealistic goals for your progress in learning the game. I made this mistake when I started out and it led to a lot of frustration and aggravation.

• *Smooth the curve by keeping statistics.* Keeping track, over time, of how you are doing in the different parts of your game helps to put the daily ups and downs in perspective. For every round of golf, for example, many golfers keep track of the following:

  • Drives in the fairway
  • Number of putts

You will probably think of other information to add to your notebook, including, possibly, the following:

- Excellent shots (with notes to help you remember them)
- Near misses (just off the green, fairway)
- Almost (should've) made putts (I have a lot of these.)
- Good shots from bunkers
- Chip-ins (shots put into the hole from off the green)

Advice from the Pro
Don't Try Too Hard

Golf is the only sport I know where trying harder seldom improves performance. Often a casual, laissez-faire, attitude is the best approach. One of the "complaints" about tour professionals is their apparently robotic emotional state. Did you ever consider that their ability to control their emotions is what makes them so good? —Mary Beth

Making mistakes less important

One of the best ways to reduce the stress associated with golf is to make poor shots and bad luck less important. There are several ways to do this; all of them involve changing the way you keep score:

- *Don't keep score.* The first way is to not keep score at all. In the beginning, this is the option you should select most of the time you are on a golf course. You should keep track of good shots and good holes, but paying attention to your total score merely increases the aggravation associated with mistakes or bad breaks.
- *Play as a member of a team, not as an individual.* Captain's Choice (or Scramble or Best Ball) is the classic format for team

Play Practice Rounds

I have found that periodic "practice rounds"—rounds in which you don't keep score, replay missed shots, and work on areas of your game that need improvement—are a good idea, no matter how proficient you have become at the game. They are especially useful after you have had a bad round or have found yourself increasingly annoyed by poor shots. They provide an opportunity to relax on the course, regain your confidence, and work on shots that may have been giving you trouble. Remember that the pros play practice rounds before every tournament.

competition. Other formats for team competition are described in "Games You Can Play" at the back of this book.

• *Match play.* If you like a bit of competition, but want to speed up the game and eliminate the misery caused by really bad holes ("horrendo holes," where you hit the ball

Advice from the Pro
You Decide When to Keep Score

Whether you choose to keep score or not is a personal preference and is up to you. Some players use the scorecard as a benchmark upon which they gauge their improvement. When I am asked my opinion about keeping score, I suggest that new golfers will *know* when that time has arrived. Don't allow yourself to be pressured into keeping score by others until you are ready. —Mary Beth into the woods or the lake a couple of times and end up with an eight or more), keep track only of which team has the best score on each hole. And, if you desire, you can pick up your ball at anytime it becomes impossible to beat the other team or player on any given hole.

• *Invent your own rules for playing and keeping score.* Unless you are playing in a tournament or maintaining a handicap, it is up to you and your playing partners to decide how you want to play and keep score.

Dealing with Embarrassment— Golf as a Performance Sport

There is no doubt that unrealistic expectations have a lot to do with occasional lapses in my good behavior on the course. Certainly, frustration and disappointment at one's performance are important contributors to the emotional side of any sport. The more competitive one's personality and the greater your investment in the game, the more your score and your apparent progress are likely to affect your reactions to your play, both on the course and off.

There is another important psychological dimension to golf, however. It is the potential, indeed likelihood, of occasional embarrassment. Only in the sport of golf is every player, from rank beginner to expert, involuntarily subject to the intense scrutiny of several other players each time he or she swings a club. When I hit a good (even moderately acceptable) tee shot, I am almost always rewarded with comments such as "Nice shot," "Good ball," or "That works." Poor shots usually elicit comforting remarks such as "Well, at least it's in the right direction" or "I think you'll find it." My most embarrassing attempts are greeted by silence, or by the polite comment, "Would you like to hit another ball?"

Often a player's reaction to an ugly shot is as much the result of embarrassment as it is disappointment or anger at oneself. In this case, it doesn't matter much whether you are keeping score or not, it's still embarrassing. The thing to remember at such times is that every single person watching your shot has been there and done the same thing many times. If it is any consolation, your terrible shot probably made everyone else feel grateful that it was you this time and not them. For this, they owe you their thanks.

How Many Tennis Jokes Do You Know?

One of the interesting things about golf is the number of jokes there are about the game. In light of the ups and downs of golf and the importance of the mental side of the game, it is probably not surprising that there are literally thousands and thousands of golf jokes. Humor is one of the best ways to manage golf's ups and downs.

Backswings

- You *never* "get it;" you just *borrow* it.
- Keep track of your good shots; forget about the poor shots.
- Keep your expectations in line with reality.
- Don't feel compelled to keep score every time you play.
- When you flub a shot, remember that it's your gift to your playing partners.
- Learn a few golf jokes.

Chapter 9

For Women (And Men Who Play Golf with Women)

Once I was giving a golf lesson to a couple of football players. They were big and muscular and lurched over the ball and gave it a whack for all it was worth. They felt like they could melt the ball with a powerful swing. I put a speed meter on them and they were swinging at fifty or sixty miles an hour and going nowhere. Then I'd swing the club, nice and smooth, and measure ninety-five miles an hour. They couldn't believe it. It went against every grain of macho man in their bodies that an old lady could generate more speed than these young, strapping boys. But they didn't understand what the golf swing should be. It's smooth, rhythmical, graceful, fluid. It's like the ballet. People need to visualize the golf swing smoothly back and accelerate smoothly through.
—Peggy Kirk Bell, *The Gift of Golf*

This chapter is for women who are learning to play golf after the age of 50 and, incidentally, any men who are fortunate enough to share this experience with them. For lots of reasons, golf is a great sport for women, but many women approach the game of golf differently from most men and have different goals and objectives. Some don't realize that golf is a sport they really can master. Fortunately, golf provides an opportunity for men and women to set their own goals and often to pursue them together. Doing so requires mutual understanding and respect for each other's needs and capabilities.

Only a small percentage of women now over 50 played any organized sports when they were in school. Before the passage of Title IX of the Education Amendments Act of 1972, which guaranteed girls in high schools and colleges the right to equal opportunity in sports, fewer than 300,000 girls were participating in high school sports, as compared with more than 3.5 million boys. This situation began to change after 1972, and by the mid-1990s, the gap between girls' and boys' participation in sports in school was narrowing. However, these gains came too late for most members of the baby boom generation. In addition to gaining physical skills, such as strength and hand-eye coordination, organized sports in school introduces many young people to the experience of competition and the importance of practice for skill development.

Of course, many women over 50 play tennis, participate regularly in activities such as walking, swimming, or cycling, or work out at a fitness center. These women are likely to see golf as a natural expansion of their existing skills. For those who haven't had the experience of playing a sport, learning to play golf can be especially rewarding.

Fortunately, golf increasingly offers many opportunities for women to learn the game. The number of instructional programs, clinics, and schools designed especially for women is growing rapidly across the country. In addition, most golf courses sponsor women's leagues that provide opportunities for regular play to women of all skill levels. Women often approach golf with relatively low expectations and are thrilled to discover that they can play the game. (Men, on the other hand, expect that learning to play golf will be easy and then are frustrated when they discover that it is much harder than it looks.) Advantage: women.

Advice from the Pro
Everyone Can Learn

Older women often come to the lesson tee with low expectations about learning to play golf. Especially if they didn't play sports while growing up, they consider themselves non-athletes. While other sports can give learners a head start at hand-eye coordination skills, it's amazing to me how many of these self-perceived non-athletes become very competent golfers. Learning to generate force and power takes some time, but I've seen countless examples of older women getting over the hump and becoming very respectable players. —Mary Beth

Golf *Is* a Women's Sport

When you stop to think about it, there are many reasons why golf should be at least as popular among women as men. The following are a few of these reasons:

• *Women tend to be more flexible than men.* Flexibility counts nearly as much as strength in the ability to hit a golf ball. Even older women can have a significant initial advantage in flexibility over men the same age.

• *Accuracy is as important as strength.* To compensate for men's greater strength, women play from the forward tees. Strength is less of a factor and accuracy becomes all-important.

• *Golf is a social game.* Golf provides an opportunity to spend several hours of quality time with people you enjoy, including family members and other women.

• *Golf rewards a calm demeanor.* The ability to stay calm and relaxed is an important element of successful golf. Most women have been practicing keeping their tempers, especially around men, their whole lives.

• *Golf is a civilized game.* Proper etiquette is an essential part of the game. This is another big plus for women.

• *Dressing nicely is part of the game.* Golf offers many opportunities to add to your wardrobe and golf fashion has improved dramatically in the past decade.

• *Travel and golf go together.* Golf provides incentives for travel to new and interesting places, as well as a diversion when you must travel for other reasons.

Advice from the Pro
Women Can Excel Around the Greens

It goes without saying that men are physically stronger than women (25 percent stronger on average); strong women golfers will never hit the ball as far as the strongest men. There is no reason, however, why women cannot excel at the short game, where strength is less of an issue. Have you ever watched a man trying to thread a needle or sew on a button? Where precision is concerned, women start with a big advantage over men. Learning to chip and putt well requires a lot of practice, but this part of the game is made for women. —Mary Beth

Learning the Game

Women are a lot less likely than men to walk on to a practice range or golf course and try to play golf without having had any instruction. After all, it is always the woman who urges her husband to stop and get directions when he is obviously lost while driving the family sedan. The inclination to seek expert assistance before proceeding is especially appropriate when learning to play golf, because it is so easy to develop bad habits by swinging a golf club without any supervision at the beginning.

Many older women take up golf for the first time with their husbands. This works fine if your husband is also starting from scratch and can restrain himself from assuming the role of instructor after the first or second lesson, which is difficult for some men. It is more problematic if your husband is already a golfer or has some experience with the game. In this case, his temptation to participate in your instruction is likely to be almost irresistible.

Advice from the Pro
Sign the Agreement

Make a pact with your husband before you start that says: "Thanks, but absolutely no advice unless I ask for it." This will lead to a longer and happier marriage and make the game more enjoyable for both of you. —Mary Beth

A great alternative (or supplement) to taking lessons with your husband is to organize a small group of women to learn the game together. You can always sign up for lessons by yourself, but you are likely to have more fun sharing the experience with friends who are also beginners. The members of your group provide mutual reinforcement and encouragement when it's needed to keep everyone going. Most important, you will already have the makings of a foursome of friends who possess roughly the same skill levels when you are ready to venture onto the golf course.

Advice from the Pro
Where Are the Women on the Practice Tee?

Several years ago, when I was teaching one evening, I looked across the practice facility and was astounded by what I saw. Of the eight people hitting practice balls, five were women. This was such an unusual occurrence that I went over and commended each of the women out there. Our practice facility is almost always 90-100 percent men, and it was so encouraging to see a majority of women on that particular evening. I hope it is the beginning of a trend. —Mary Beth

Practice

Just as women are *more* likely than men to start golf with an instructional program, they are much *less* likely than men to spend any time on the practice tee. This is especially the case among older women, many of whom take up golf to keep their husbands company or to participate in social groups at their club or in their community. When they play well or happen to hit a good shot they are pleased, but only rarely do they work on improving their skills in any systematic way.

If this approach to the game of golf works for you, don't let anyone pressure you into changing it. However, keep the following ideas in mind:

- Even modest improvements in basic skills can make golf a lot more fun to play.
- Anyone can and will improve with regular practice.
- There are ways to make practice both sociable and fun.

Make the Most of Your Golf Group

Include regular practice sessions in the schedule of activities for your golf learning group. In the beginning, for example, you might try to schedule two group lessons per week, each followed by a half hour on the driving range. After a total of six lessons, you might slip to one lesson a week (followed by practice), one session just for practice, and one nine-hole round of golf (using Mary Beth's *New Golfer Rules*). If you and your friends are able to follow such a routine for three months, I am willing to bet that you will all be hitting shots with a fair amount of consistency. And, you will have laid the foundation for a great deal of future enjoyment of the game of golf.

Exercise

If you have been running, playing tennis or some other sport, working out, or otherwise staying physically active, getting into shape to play golf should not present any problems for you. Remember that golf is a multi-plane sport in which flexibility is as important as strength. Thus, stretching is particularly important, especially when warming up before a round of golf. It never ceases to astonish me how many men and women walk up to the first tee and hit their first shot without even taking a practice swing, much less stretching or loosening up by swinging a golf club. You wouldn't start a tennis match without hitting a few balls to loosen up; why would you expect to be able to hit a golf ball well without warming up?

If golf is your first major physical activity since you left school or college, you should pay attention to the exercise advice in "Get in Shape for Golf" at the back of this book to strengthen and protect the muscles in the center of your body (the core), improve your balance, and increase leg, shoulders, arms, and hand strength.

Advice from the Pro
Strength Training Does Work

I recently had an older woman pupil who wore elbow braces and wristbands and always seemed to have an injured body part. However, after six months of a supervised cardio and weight program, she no longer complains about any aching body parts. She gives 100 percent credit to the weight program and, as an added benefit, the distance of her shots has improved significantly. Weight training has been proven to have positive effects well into one's 70s and 80s. So, get on the bandwagon and enjoy the improvements to your golf game, not to mention your overall health. —Mary Beth

Advice from the Pro
Keep that Rear End Out

In our culture, women have been trained since an early age to suck in their stomach and keep their hips tucked under. This is a big challenge for me in teaching the correct golf posture to older women. Maintaining the proper tilt in a golf swing is not a natural thing for many women. As a result, many novice women start their swing and immediately straighten up and tuck their hips under. Ladies, please remember to keep your rear end out. If you don't stand up tall on your backswing, you won't have to bend down to hit the golf ball. As Peggy Kirk Bell says: "Turn and return." —Mary Beth

Take that Divot—Overcoming
Fears of Damaging the Golf Course

When you watch a golf tournament on television, you will notice that players frequently take large "divots" (saucer- and sometimes dinner plate-sized pieces of dirt and sod) when they hit the ball. This happens because in a good golf swing the club is descending when it strikes the ball. *After the club hits the ball*, the arc of the swing causes the club to dig into the grass, producing a divot. Many new golfers, especially women, are afraid of "hurting the golf course" when they swing at the ball. They try to scoop the ball off the grass without hitting the ground and end up hitting just the top of the ball, causing in to bounce along the ground.

The bottom line is that it is often necessary to take a divot to hit the ball solidly. Overcoming your concerns about damaging the course is the first step. Divots are a normal part of the game and most courses ask golfers either to replace the divots they make or pour a mixture of sand and grass seed on the holes dug by their clubs. Think of your divots as helping to grow new grass.

Who Should You Play with

As more women take up golf, the range of options women have for playing partners is increasing rapidly in many areas. In the beginning, it makes sense to play with people who are learning at the same time you are. If you are taking lessons with your husband and you can restrain him from constantly giving you advice, there is nothing wrong with playing as a couple. If you know another couple whose skills are at more or less the same level, a foursome in which the men ride together and women share their own cart often works very well. If you can organize your own group of women, ideally to both play and practice together, this is a great way to have fun and improve your skills. Among the quickest ways to gain experience is to play with a friend as a twosome when the course is not crowded, and you can each hit multiple balls, re-hit missed shots, and practice putts on each green.

Women's leagues

Many golf courses now sponsor regular leagues for women. The league my wife plays in every Monday morning is organized into four flights to accommodate players of varying skill levels and features a different format each week for added interest and fun. The formats vary so everyone has a chance to win sometimes, not just the best golfers. Examples include scoring only odd or even holes or just putts, limiting players to three or four clubs, and allowing each player two mulligans during the round. Pins are awarded for birdies, and there are end-of-season tournaments in several formats with winners from each flight and a tournament for the 12 players with the best scores during the season. The season ends with an awards luncheon every fall.

Many women play *only* in women's leagues because they don't feel comfortable playing with golfers, especially men, whose skill levels are much higher. Women's leagues provide a particularly supportive environment for older women who regularly shoot in the 60s or 70s for nine holes. They count every shot, enjoy the company, and have a lot of fun.

Playing with men

Some women like playing golf with men, while others are more comfortable playing with other women golfers. My wife and I took up golf at the same time and we still enjoy playing a round of golf together. However, she also looks forward to playing with her friends, women who value the social aspects of the game highly and may not care much about their score. Men tend to take the game more seriously, especially when they are playing one (or more) of the competitive games that golf offers. I anguish over missed opportunities, while my wife simply moves on when she flubs a shot. Among many other things, she has taught me that no one else really wants to know how disappointed I am by my mistakes.

Many men also have a hard time resisting what sometimes seems like a natural-born tendency to give advice to any woman they see on a golf course. This is especially true of husbands and wives, and it has little to do with the man's level of expertise. Men rarely give unsolicited advice to another male golfer, but women often bring out all of their instructional instincts. Having personally committed this sin, I speak with authority when I urge new women golfers to politely, but firmly, remind their male playing partners that if they want advice on any aspect of the game, they will be sure to ask for it. As for men, if you enjoy and want to continue playing golf with your wife or any other women golfers, curb your urge to offer advice.

Mixing business and golf

The game of golf has always played an important role in business, politics, and the professions for many golfers. What other activity can you imagine where it is possible to spend four or five relaxed, uninterrupted, hours in the company of two or three business colleagues, existing or prospective clients, or other influential people. Until recently, unfortunately, these opportunities were available primarily to men.

As the number of women in positions of responsibility in all areas of society has increased, so too have opportunities for women to mix business and golf. The baby boomers are the first generation in which a significant proportion of women have succeeded in combining high-level careers with family responsibilities. As their children go off to college, a growing number of women are making golf a part of their professional life, playing golf with both men and other women executives. There is now an Executive Women's Golf Association with 20,000 members and 115 chapters (see "Resources" at the back of this book). Corporate golf outings that a decade or two ago were comprised entirely of men now include many more women. For their part, men are discovering the competitive advantage of having a competent woman golfer as part of their foursome in a scramble format (women play from the forward tees and often have a very strong short game).

A Word about Golf Communities

An increasing number of women take up golf for the first time when they move to a golf community with their husbands. Many of these women have had very successful careers, but have been too busy juggling career and family responsibilities to take the time to learn how to play golf. Because so much of the social life in such communities revolves around golf, these women often feel great pressure to learn how to play golf quickly. If their husband already plays golf, the pressure can be especially great. To make matters worse, these successful women are accustomed to being very good at everything they do. Learning to play golf can come as a shock.

If you find yourself in this position, take a deep breath and tell your husband and your friends that you want to take your time learning the game and you will let them know when you feel comfortable about playing with their groups. If you can, form your own group of women who are at your level, and develop a play and practice routine like the one described above. Do your best to avoid playing with more experienced golfers, no matter how hard they try to persuade you, until you are satisfied with your game. If one doesn't already exist, see if you can get your community to organize a program like Mary Beth's Stoney Creek 9-Hole Golf League for New Women Golfers (see sidebar page 151).

Backswings

• Even if you don't think of yourself as an athlete, you can learn to play golf.

• Golf is a women's sport.

• Organize a group of your friends to learn, practice, and play golf together.

• Practice is fun and essential for improvement.

• Don't let yourself be pressured into playing on a golf course, especially with men, until you are ready.

• Don't let your husband give you advice unless you ask for it.

• Join a women's league if you can find one. If not, encourage your teaching professional to organize one.

• Don't worry about damaging the grass with your clubs.

Advice from the Pro
Introducing New Women Golfers
to the Course

My objective with my Stoney Creek 9-Hole Golf League for New Women Golfers is to help women "get over the hump"—whether this means feeling confident enough to actually start playing golf, starting to keep score, learning to play with strangers, or generally feeling more confident and comfortable just being on the golf course.

This league is intended to be new-golfer friendly and noncompetitive—the goal is to have fun, make new friends, enjoy the great outdoors, and improve each woman's playing ability. The women themselves have a free hand in designing the way of playing that works best for them. They may choose whether to keep score and whether to tee up the ball in the fairway—whatever gives them confidence and success.

I generally play a few holes with each group and keep rotating from group to group. During play, the women are free to address any special needs and ask questions about rules, etiquette, course management, and the like. I am happy to help with alignment, reading the greens, uneven lies, club selection, and other strategy questions; however, the golf course is not the place to work on specific swing mechanics. Because time is so often cited as a reason women give up the game, I suggest they make it a goal to always play nine holes in two hours.

Following are some of the suggestions I make about different ways to play:

1. Play Captain's Choice (Scramble) format. Each player hits from the tee box, then the best shot is chosen and each

player hits from that spot. Continue in this manner until the ball is in the hole.

2. Play from special tees: Play the par 5s from the 250-yard marker, the par 4s from the 200-yard marker, play from the forward tees on the par 3s.

3. Allow "do-overs" (or floating mulligans); for example, one for a tee shot, one for a chip or pitch, and one for a putt. Before you begin, determine how many of each to allow during the round (making sure that you are not holding up play with these extra practice shots).

4. If you are playing in a twosome, play a type of individual scramble game by playing two balls from the position of each of the best of your own shots. This is a great way to get extra practice on the course as long as you are not holding up other golfers.

5. Play your first ball from the tee box, then pick up your ball and proceed to the 100-yard marker and play in from there.

6. Play the "Texas Scramble" format, in which the best drive of the group is selected and then each member of the group plays their own ball from that spot to the green.

7. When you feel ready to start keeping score, allow yourself three shots on par 3s, four shots on par 4s, and five shots on par 5s to get close to the green. If you're struggling, simply pick up your golf ball after the allotted number of swings, place it on the edge of the green, and then chip and putt to finish the hole from there.

If you choose to keep score, make "double par" the maximum on any given hole. As you improve, make triple bogey the maximum. Circle your score on the scorecard every time you invoke this rule. You'll see progress when you have fewer, or better yet, no circles on the scorecard.

—Mary Beth

Resources

Games to Play

One of the most notable things about golf is the number and variety of different games that golfers play. The format of golf is ideally suited to a seemingly infinite variety of competitions for both individuals and teams. These range from the simplest and silliest wagers (for example, anyone who skips their ball across a pond or who makes par after hitting a tree gets to deduct a stroke) to complicated team competitions in which team members change during a round, bets may double or triple, and individual handicaps are taken into account. Entire books have been written about the games of golf and we provide references to several in "Books about Golf" on page 170. To whet your appetite, some examples follow.

Match Play

The most common format for social golf is *match play*. Whether you are playing as an individual or as a member of a team, the only thing that counts in match play is the number of holes that you or your team win. The individual or team with the lowest score on each hole wins that hole (ties either don't count or they are carried over to the next hole); whoever wins the most holes wins the match. The majority of the games that people have devised are based on match play and most of these games involve teams.

Stroke Play

In stroke play, the total number of strokes at the end of the round or tournament (which might be several rounds) determines who wins. The winner may be based on *low gross* (total strokes) or *low net* (total strokes, less handicap allowance).

A Few of the Most Popular Unofficial Games

Captain's Choice, Scramble, Best Ball

The most popular format for charity tournaments and other events involving players of different skill levels is called Captain's Choice, Scramble or Best Ball. In this format, after everyone hits their tee shot, the best shot is selected and everyone hits their second shot from this spot. This procedure continues until the ball is into the hole. It can be played as stroke competition, or in two- or four-person teams in match play. This relatively pressure-free format is great fun for everyone, especially for new golfers.

Better Ball

Better ball is a typical match play competition, usually pitting two members of a foursome against the other two. The better score of the two players on each team counts on each hole and the lowest score wins the hole. Ties don't count, or they are carried over to the next hole. Handicaps are usually taken into account. (If one or more players doesn't have a handicap, teams are either balanced to take account of players' abilities, or strokes may be given to players in advance.) A scoring variation gives an additional point to a team that has both the lowest individual score and the lowest combined score on each hole.

Skins

This is the popular game that you can watch the pros play on television at Thanksgiving. The player who wins a hole outright on a net basis (that is, after adjustments for handicaps) gets a "skin." Skins have a constant value decided by the players; for example, $1 per player (with a foursome, the winner of a hole nets a $3 profit). If there is a tie among any of the players for the lowest score on a hole, the skin carries over to the next hole, which is played for two skins. If that hole is tied, the skins carry over again, and so on, until one of the players wins a hole outright. One of the interesting things about the game is that you can find yourself rooting for one of your competitors to make a shot that will tie the lowest score on a hole so that the skin will carry over to the next hole.

Nassau

The best-known wager in golf is a Nassau. The Nassau may be set at any amount of money, but $2 is typical. Again, the game is for two-person teams and the members of the team that wins the most holes on the front nine each get $2. Another $2 per team member is won on the back nine, and a third $2 is paid out for the most holes won overall. A total of $6 therefore is at stake for each player *unless additional bets are made during the course of the round*, which typically happens automatically when one team falls two holes down. This is called a "press," and each press or double press increases the stakes. Determine the rules are for presses before you agree to play this game; it can get expensive.

Wolf

Wolf is a game for three or four players and is played in the match play, better-ball format. Handicaps are used. Players take turns teeing off first according to a pre-established rotation (each player in a foursome will tee off first four times in the first sixteen holes). The player who tees off first is the wolf and may select any of the other players as his or her partner, or may choose to play against all of the others as the lone wolf. The only catch is that the wolf must choose a partner immediately after that person's tee shot (he can wait until the fourth player tees off, but then must either choose that player as his partner or play against all of the others). Lone wolves win double points. High handicap players with a good short game will be in high demand as partners.

Bingo, Bango, Bongo

In Bingo, Bango, Bongo, three points are awarded on each hole (again, the value of a point can be set at any amount; 25 cents works for my group): One point is awarded for the first ball on the green, one point for the ball closest to the pin after all players are on the green (no matter how many strokes it took to get there), and one point for the first ball in the hole. This is a great game for new golfers because, as you will quickly see, the rules compensate well even for big differences in skill levels.

One Club

In this game, everyone is limited to one club. You may be surprised to discover how well you play using only one club for all of your shots. Variations, of course, are one club and a putter, or two clubs, etc.

Side Bets (Also Called Garbage Bets)

Almost anything you can think of happening on the golf course can be turned into a side bet and awarded points during a round. Among the most common are the following:

Chippies. Making a single shot up (onto the green) and down (into the hole) from anywhere around the green.

Sandies. Getting up-and-down in two shots from a bunker.

Flaggies. Hitting your tee shot on any hole to within a flag-stick's distance from the cup.

Froggies. Skipping a shot across a water hazard.

Gurglies/Splashies. Making par (or bogey) after hitting into a water hazard.

Barkies. Making par (or bogey) after hitting a tree.

Greenies. Closest tee shot to the hole (on the green) on par 3s. Points may carry over to the next par 3 if no player is on the green with his or her first shot.

Exercises for Golfers

Mary Beth and I had a debate about whether to include a section on exercise in this book. She felt strongly that we should; exercise is essential for maintaining flexibility and building core body strength, both of which are necessary for avoiding injury and improving performance. I countered that most of the recreational golfers I have encountered don't even bother to warm up before a round, much less stick to a regular exercise routine. The new golfers who do exercise regularly don't need us to tell them how important it is to their game and those who don't exercise won't follow our advice.

She insisted that we owe it to prospective new golfers over 50, especially those who haven't been especially active in recent years, to point out the benefits of preparing yourself physically to play golf, as well as the risks of not doing so. Of course, she is right. So here goes.

Why exercise is important for learning and playing golf

People over the age of 50 don't like to admit it, but they can't do all of the things they could do when they were 25 or, at least, as well as they did them when they were younger. Strength and flexibility decline with age, while susceptibility to injury increases. Both of these trends accelerate after age 50. Active participation in sports and/or a regular exercise routine, such as running or fitness training can slow the rate of deterioration, but cannot totally prevent the inevitable. If, like many older men and women, you are taking up golf after a decade or two of relative inactivity, it is especially important for you to understand the particular stresses that golf puts upon the body.

Two things about golf underscore the importance of physical conditioning—both between rounds and in preparation for play.

- Peak physical exertion in golf is intermittent rather than continuous.

Unlike tennis or swimming or cycling, golfers actually engage in the principal physical act of golf—that is, swinging a golf club—only a small number of times during a round of golf. The rest of the time, they are walking, riding in a golf cart, or standing around waiting for someone else to swing a club. It is more difficult in golf than in most other sports to get into the flow of the game, keep muscles warm, and sustain the flexibility on which the swing depends.

• The golf swing involves multiple muscle groups and significant twisting of the body, including the spine and most joints.

There are relatively few other movements in most people's lives that generate as much stress on all parts of the body as the golf swing. Raking leaves in the fall or shoveling snow come close.

When muscles, tendons, and ligaments are cold and inflexible there is greater strain on all parts of the body, performance suffers, and the risk of injury increases.

There are a few simple things you can do to help cope with the physical demands of golf, while also significantly increasing your ability to play the game.

The following are two keys to golf fitness:

• Stretch to maintain flexibility
• Strengthen the body core

Stretch to Maintain Flexibility

It took me some time to fully appreciate the fact that a powerful golf swing does not depend primarily on how hard you swing the club, using the smaller muscles in your arms and wrists. Appearances notwithstanding, most of the power in a good golf swing is generated by the large muscles at the center of your body.

During the golf swing, your body is *both pivoting and twisting*, first, turning in one direction (during the backswing) and then turning in the opposite direction (in the downswing and follow-through). The more flexible your body is, the more rotation you can achieve, and the more power you are able to generate.

Studies have shown that the biggest difference between amateur golfers and professionals is in the amount of trunk rotation. Older and less skilled players get, on average, *less than half* the trunk rotation of skilled, younger players. With decreased flexibility, there is a temptation to depend more on smaller muscles to achieve the same clubhead speed, i.e., to try to hit the ball harder. This is a prescription for flubbed shots, and it puts more stress on your muscles, thereby increasing fatigue and the overall risk of injury.

Strengthen the Core

The large muscles that control the rotation of the body during the golf swing are located in or near the center of your body: the chest (pectorals), stomach (abdominals), hips (abductors and extensors), rear end (gluteus), and upper legs (quadriceps). In addition to helping guide the golf club along the proper path to the ball, these muscles also are responsible for protecting your body's bones and joints from the stress produced by twisting and turning. The stronger these muscles are, the better your posture will be, the more power you can generate, the more control you will have over your swing, and the less likely you are to incur physical problems with your shoulders, back, hips and knees.

Some Key Exercises You Can Do

There is no way to prevent the gradual decline in strength and flexibility that occurs with age. However, regular exercises of the key muscles groups in your shoulders, chest, torso, back, and legs can help slow the process. While staying in shape is a challenge for everyone over the age of 50, there are significant differences among individuals in both strength and flexibility and the relationship between the two. We strongly recommend that you consult with a trainer or physical therapist who can develop a regular program of exercises tailored to fit your specific needs.

Having a few exercises that you do regularly is worth far more than a comprehensive routine that you remember to do once a month. On the next few pages are ten exercises to get you started, along with a two-minute warm-up routine to use before you tee off.

Flexibility

Trunk stretch*

Lying on your back (you can do this exercise and some of the others below—indicated by an asterisk—before you get out of bed in the morning), pull your knees up until your thighs form a 90-degree angle with your torso. Then, rotate your knees (together) down to one side until they nearly touch the ground (or the bed) and hold for 3 to 5 seconds, keeping your shoulders flat. Bring your knees back to vertical and then rotate them down to the other side. Work up to 5 to 10 stretches on each side.

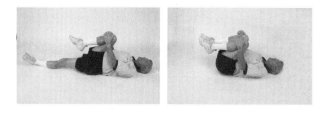

Knees to chest*

Still lying on your back, alternate bringing one knee, and then the other, all the way to your chest and holding each with your arms for 20 seconds. Keep the other leg flat. Repeat this movement three times for each knee. Then, pull both knees to your chest and hold for 20 seconds. Repeat three times.

Hamstring stretches*

While lying on your back, grasp one leg behind the thigh and pull that leg toward your chest, keeping the leg as straight as possible. Alternate legs and hold each stretch for 20 seconds. Repeat five times for each leg.

Side stretch

Stand with your hands on your hips and bend to the left until you feel the stretch in the muscles on your right side. Hold for 20 seconds. Do 3 to 5 stretches on each side.

Strengthening the Core

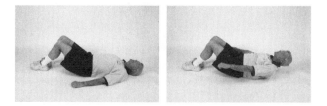

Abdominal curl (abdominal muscles)*
While lying on your back, rotate your hips so that your lower back is pressing down on the floor (or your bed). Then lift your shoulders just enough to increase the involvement of your abdominal muscles. Hold for five seconds. Work up to 20 repetitions.

Opposite arm and leg lift (extensors in back)
Positioned on your hands and knees, alternate lifting one arm and the opposite leg until they extend straight out from your body. Hold each lift 3 to 5 seconds. Work up to 20 repetitions. If you have trouble maintaining your balance, this exercise can be done on top of an exercise ball.

The plank or bridge (abdominals and gluteus)
Support your body on your elbows and toes, keeping the body as straight as possible (try not to let your rear end stick up

into the air). Hold for 20 to 40 seconds. Work up to 4 repetitions, holding each 30 seconds, with a 30-second rest between each repetition. This will be difficult at first.

Side leg lift (hip abductors)*
While lying on your side, lift one leg as far as you can lift it, keeping it straight. Hold each lift for 10 to 20 seconds. Work up to five lifts on each side.

Wall squats, with or without ball (quadriceps)
With your back braced against a wall (or door) for balance, work up to 20 to 25 squats. This can be done with an exercise ball between your back and the wall.

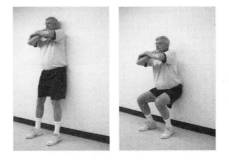

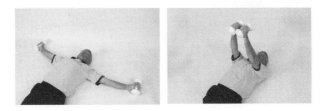

Chest muscles (pectorals)*
While lying on your back with your arms extended straight out (snow angel position), lift both arms straight up until your hands come together holding a weight in each hand. Start with one or two pounds and work up to 3 to 4 pounds.

Warm-up Stretches: Two Minutes on the First Tee

Hamstring stretch

Place your hands on your knees (to take the strain off of your back) and bend forward with your legs straight until you feel the stretch in your hamstrings. Hold for 20 seconds. Repeat.

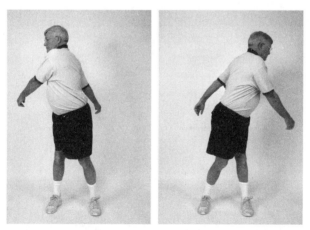

Trunk rotation

With your legs slightly apart and your arms hanging loosely at your sides, rotate your upper body as far as it will go, first to one side and then the other, allowing your arms to swing freely to increase the stretch at the end of each turn. Continue for 20 seconds.

Swing stretch

Hold a golf club with your arms behind your back (see above) and take your golf stance with your feet spread apart and your body bent forward. Simulate the golf swing by rotating first to one side and then the other, pointing the end of the club toward the ground on the inside of each turn. Continue for 20 seconds.

Shoulder stretch

Repeat the previous rotational stretches with the golf club behind your shoulders (20 seconds).

Swing two clubs

Take the two heaviest clubs—sand wedge and pitching wedge—and swing them back and forth as you would in a golf swing, beginning with very short swings and gradually increasing the length of your swing (20 seconds).

How to Select an Instructor

The following are some considerations involved in choosing a golf teacher:

- Membership in the Professional Golfers' Association (PGA) or the Ladies Professional Golf Association (LPGA). There are excellent golf instructors who are not members of the PGA or LPGA, but association with the PGA or LPGA is an indicator of a long-term professional commitment to the game, along with rigorous qualifications.
- Extensive experience teaching older adults, both men and women.
- Location at a golf course or club near your home or office that has a good practice facility, including driving range, putting green, and areas for practicing chipping, pitching and bunker play. Many people attend golf schools or take lessons from the resident professional when they are on vacation at golf resorts. While this is an excellent way to combine instruction, practice, and the enjoyment of playing a new course, convenience to a local course is essential to facilitate practice and to promote the develop-ment of a long-term relationship with an instructor who understands your particular needs and keeps track of your progress.
- Someone who stresses the fundamentals of the swing.
- If you are a visual learner, someone who can provide you with access to video technology.
- A person with whom you have a good rapport, is supportive of your goals, and who makes you feel at home on the practice tee.
- Someone who encourages you to practice and helps you develop a practice routine that you will be able to stick with, including helping you to find practice and playing partners.

Finding the right teacher is similar to finding a good physician. For recommendations, you may begin by asking friends who play golf at courses convenient to you. The PGA and LPGA provide lists of their members who are teaching professionals in your area on their websites (see below), and the major publications—*Golf Magazine, Golf Digest,* and *Golf for Women*—publish annual lists of the top 50 or 100 instructors, by region.

Don't feel any obligation to the first person who gives you a lesson; in fact, it is often useful to take lessons from several teachers in order to compare their approaches. You may decide to begin with small group lessons (especially, if you can organize a group of your friends to learn, practice, and play together), but periodic individual lessons are a good idea.

Books for Golfers

Chi Chi's Golf Games You Gotta Play: Shots and Side Bets to Outscore and Outshark your Opponents, by Chi Chi Rodriguez and John Anderson. Human Kinetics, Champaign, Illinois, 2003. The authoritative and humorous guide to the betting games of golf.

Cindy Reid's Ultimate Guide to Golf for Women, by Cindy Reid and Steve Eubanks. Atria Books, New York, 2003.

Dave Pelz's Short Game Bible: Master the Finesse Swing and Lower Your Score, by Dave Pelz, with James A. Frank. Doubleday, New York, 1999. Everything you need to know about the short game.

Golf for Dummies: A Reference for the Rest of Us, by Gary McCord. Wiley Publishing Co., Hoboken, NJ. Latest edition, 2006. A readable, complete summary of all aspects of the game of golf written by a former PGA Tour champion and current CBS golf analyst.

Golf is Not a Game of Perfect, by Dr. Bob Rotella, with Bob Cullen. Simon and Schuster, New York, 1995. The first of several excellent books on the mental aspects of golf by the former Director of Sports Psychology at the University of Virginia.

How I Play Golf, by Tiger Woods, with the editors of *Golf Digest.* Warner Books, New York, 2001. The richly illustrated classic by the most famous golfer in the world.

The Little Red Book of Golf: Lessons and Teachings from a Lifetime in Golf, by Harvey Pennick, with Bud Schrake. Fireside Books, Simon and Schuster, New York, 1992. The classic collection of golf stories and wisdom from one of golf's greatest teachers.

Newton on the Tee: A Good Walk Through the Science of Golf, by

John Zumerchik. Simon and Schuster, New York, 2002. An in-depth look at the science underlying golf, written by a physicist and former editor of the *Encyclopedia of Sports Science*.

Rock Solid Golf: A Foundation for a Lifetime, by Dana Rader. Walkabout Press, Charlotte, North Carolina, 2003. One of the clearest presentations of the fundamentals of golf written by one of the foremost woman golf instructors.

The Unplayable Lie: The Untold Story of Women and Discrimination in American Golf, by Marcia Chambers. Pocket Books, New York, 1996.

Venus on the Fairway: Creating a Swing—And a Game That Works for Women, by Debbie Steinbach. McGraw Hill, New York, 2001.

Internet Sites of Interest to Golfers

golf.com The most comprehensive site for information about golf on the internet.

golfdigest.com From the publishers of *Golf Digest*.

golfonline.com From the publishers of *Golf Magazine* and *Golf Week*.

pga.com The official website of the Professional Golf Association.

lpga.com The official site of the Ladies Professional Golf Association.

golfforwomen.com The site of *Golf for Women* magazine.

ewga.com The official site of the Executive Women's Golf Association. Organized in 1991, it has 20,000 members and 115 chapters.

Golf Schools

Almost every golf course offers instruction by the resident professional or teaching staff. Golf schools and organized instructional programs for men and women at all levels can be found at most golf resorts, many golf clubs, and countless other locations throughout the country. Instructional programs conducted in locations with extensive practice facilities—including areas for practicing bunker play and the short game—are harder to come by. Here is a sampling of the best.

Faldo Institute by Marriott. Golf instruction built around extensive practice facilities at four locations: Orlando, Florida; Palm Desert, California; Atlantic City, New Jersey; and Marco Island, Florida.

Pine Needles Lodge and Country Club, Southern Pines, North Carolina. World famous golf school, with exceptional practice facilities. The Learning Center and *Golfaris* for women only, although programs for couples are offered.

Grand Cypress Academy of Golf, Orlando, Florida. Computerized instruction, and practice holes in a 25-acre complex. (grandcypress.com)

Kiawah Island Golf Academy, Kiawah Island, Georgia. Indoor video analysis studio, practice bunkers, covered range.

PGA Learning Center, Port St. Lucie, Florida. This 35-acre golf park offers one of the largest and most advanced teaching and practice facilities in the world. State-of-the-art video and computer analyses and areas devoted to all aspects of the game. (pga.com)

Pinehurst Golf Academy, Pinehurst, North Carolina. This golf school is associated with the famous Pinehurst Golf Resort. State-of-the-art instructional facilities and eight courses to play.

Cog Hill Golf and Country Club, Lemont, Illinois (near Chicago). Driving range/learning center with grass tees and well-groomed, short-game practice area.

Ping Learning Center, Karsten Golf Course, Arizona State University, Tempe, Arizona. Short game practice facility and state-of-the-art video analysis. (asukarsten.com)

McGetrick Golf Academy, Green Valley Ranch Golf Club, Denver, Colorado. Instruction in all aspects of the game, plus a new nine-hole short course that is perfect for beginners.

Capitol City Golf School, Washington, D.C. Economical year-round individual and group instruction programs. Two nine-hole and one 18-hole courses. Heated driving range for winter practice, including dedicated practice holes.

The First Tee, Richmond and Chesterfield, Virginia. Great playing and practice facilities, ideal for juniors, women, and those over 50. (thefirstteerichmondchesterfield.org)

A Glossary of Golf Terms

Ace: a hole in one. This is a big deal. Many golf clubs keep a plaque with names of golfers who score a hole-in-one. Custom requires you to buy a round of drinks for everyone who is around the clubhouse following the round.

Address: taking your position before swinging the golf club, including grip, posture, stance, ball position, and alignment to the target. Technically (according to the rules), this is the point at which you have taken your stance and grounded your club (except in a hazard), prior to initiating your backswing.

Approach: a shot hit toward the green from anywhere on the course, except from the tee.

Apron: the closely mown area immediately surrounding the putting surface (also called the fringe).

Away: refers to the ball farthest from the hole, which is customarily played first.

Back Nine or Back Side: the second nine-holes of a round; holes 10–18.

Best Ball: a game in which only the best score among two, or more, players on a team is counted on each hole.

Birdie: one stroke under par on any hole. Making "birdie" is a pretty big deal for new golfers over 50.

Bite: a command often used wishfully to urge the ball to stop rolling once it hits the green; the term refers to the desire for a backward spin that causes a ball to slow down or stop abruptly once it lands on the green. Golf balls rarely listen to such commands.

Bogey: one stroke over par on any hole.

Break: the direction in which, and the degree to which a putt will curve as it rolls toward the hole, due to variations in the surface and slope of the green.

Bunker (Sand Trap): a hazard on the golf course; usually a depression in the ground filled with sand. Bunkers vary greatly in size, shape, type of sand, and difficulty of escaping from them.

Carry: the distance the ball travels in the air after being hit, an important consideration when a water hazard is in front of you.

Casual Water: a temporary accumulation of water on the course. If your ball is in such an area (or you must stand in such an area to hit your ball), a drop is permitted without any penalty.

Chunk: a poor shot resulting from hitting the ground behind the ball.

Compression: the flattening of the ball that occurs when it is struck by the club.

Course Rating: a numerical rating (expressed in strokes and decimals of a stroke) that evaluates the playing difficulty of a course compared with other rated courses. The course rating is more refined than par and is based on both yardage and the expected score of a scratch (expert) golfer.

Cup: the receptacle in the hole that holds the flagstick in place and helps keep the hole from collapsing.

Dance Floor: slang for the putting green.

Divot: chunk of turf displaced by a golfer's club during the swing. Most golf courses ask golfers to replace their divots or fill the holes with a combination of sand and grass seed (usually from a container attached to the golf cart).

Dogleg: a hole that bends left or right before you reach the green.

Draw: a shot that curves slightly left (for a right-handed golfer).

Driving Range: a golf practice facility that enables players to hit real golf balls with any of the clubs in their bag, including the driver.

Drive: shot from the tee (except on par-3 holes).

Drop: method for putting a ball back into play after it has been moved or replaced in accordance with the rules. Stand erect, extend your arm, and drop the ball from shoulder height.

Eagle: two shots under par on any hole. A hole-in-one on a par three hole is an eagle.

Fairway (Short Grass): The closely mown area between the teeing ground and the green. Every golfer's goal is to keep his or her ball in the fairway.

Fairway Wood: "wooden" clubs other than the driver. All large-headed clubs today are made with metal alloys, so such clubs are also called "metalwoods" or "fairway metals."

Fat: to hit the ground before striking the ball with the club. Fat shots don't travel as far as balls that are hit cleanly. Similar to a "chunk."

Flagstick (Pin): tall, thin, removable pole with a flag attached at the top; it is positioned in the center of the cup on the green and indicates the location of the hole (which is changed every day on most courses).

Fore: shout to warn other players of an errant shot headed in their direction.

Fried Egg: slang description of a ball buried in the sand.

Fringe (Apron; Collar): the very closely mown grass immediately surrounding the green.

Front nine: the first nine-holes of a round; holes 1–9.

Gimmie: a short putt that is conceded so that the player does not have to putt; this is often done to speed up the pace of play. Technically, not permitted by the rules.

Green: the putting surface.

Green in Regulation (GIR): the number of shots it should take an expert golfer to arrive on the green (e.g., on a par-4 hole, it should take an expert golfer two shots to reach the green, leaving two putts for a par; taking two shots to reach the green on a par-4 hole is considered hitting the green in regulation).

Greens Fee: the cost to play a round (9 or 18 holes) of golf.

Gross Score: the total number of strokes taken by a player in a round of golf (before any handicap allowance is deducted).

Ground the Club: touching or resting the club on the grass (ground) behind the ball at address; "grounding the club" is prohibited in hazards, such as bunkers.

Ground Under Repair: an area on the course that is marked (usually by white paint) to indicate that repairs are taking place; no penalty is incurred if your ball lands in such an area. You may drop your ball within one club length of your nearest point of relief.

Go to School: to watch another player's putt if it is on a similar line to the hole as your ball. The purpose is to better gauge how hard and on what line to hit your putt.

Hazard: bunkers (sand) or water (except temporary accumulations) on the course.

Handicap: the number of strokes over par a particular golfer is expected to score, on average, for 18 holes.

Honor: the right earned by a player to tee off first because of having the lowest score on the previous hole. This privilege carries over until another player earns it by achieving a lower score on a succeeding hole.

Hook: a shot that curves sharply left (for a right-handed golfer).

Hosel: the part of the club between the shaft and the clubhead.

Hybrid: a club incorporating features of both an iron and a fairway metal, designed to get the ball up in the air quickly. Many golfers, especially those over 50, are replacing their long irons (numbers 3, 4, and 5) with hybrids.

Improve Your Lie: moving the position of your ball within a short distance in your own fairway, typically one club length, to make it easier to hit. Often permitted by local rules during the winter or when the condition of the course is poor. (See **Winter Rules.**)

Lag: a long putt (or pitch or chip shot) intended to stop close to the hole.

Lateral Hazard: water hazard parallel to the fairway and designated by red stakes. Other areas (for example, environmentally sensitive areas) may be designated as lateral hazards by local rules. Balls hit into lateral hazards incur a one-stroke penalty.

Lay Up: a conservative shot hit deliberately to avoid potential trouble ahead.

Lie: the position of your ball when it comes to rest after your shot. Also refers to the angle of the sole of the club relative to the shaft.

Loft: the degree of angle of the clubface. The higher the degree, the higher the expected trajectory of the ball when hit. Putters have the least loft; sand and/or lob wedges have the most.

Line: intended path of the ball to the hole, usually in the context of putting.

Local Rules: special rules established by course members, the course rules committee, or the club professional.

Long Irons: the 1- to 4-irons, which are the most difficult to hit. Many golfers are replacing them with fairway woods (metalwoods) or hybrids.

Loose Impediments: natural, unattached, and unembedded objects, such as stones, leaves, branches, twigs, insects, and the like. Provided you are not in a hazard, they may be removed without penalty prior to your shot.

LPGA: Ladies Professional Golf Association.

Marshal (Ranger): roving official responsible for player assistance and for ensuring that players adhere to course rules regarding carts and maintain the pace of play.

Match Play: two sides (teams or individuals) compete to see who wins the most holes.

Metalwood: fairway wood (or driver) made of metal, as all modern clubs are.

Mulligan: a free shot (do-over), usually on the first tee, especially when a practice range is not available or if time does not permit a warm-up. **Floating mulligans** are also sometimes sold in charity tournaments or incorporated for fun in local league competitions. There is no such thing in the official rules of golf.

Nassau: a bet on who wins the front nine, back nine, and the full 18; the best known wager in golf.

Net Score: score for a hole or round after deduction of a player's handicap.

OB: out-of-bounds.

Open Clubface: clubface aligned to the right of the target (for right-handed golfers).

Open Stance: the foot closer to the target at address is farther away from the line to the target than the back foot; tends to cause left-to-right ball flight.

Par: the score an expert player is expected to make on a hole, either a 3, 4, or 5.

Pace of Play: the average amount of time a foursome is expected to take to play each hole; usually no more than 15 minutes.

PGA: Professional Golfer's Association.

Play Through: invitation to the group behind you when your group is playing slowly and the hole ahead is open.

Preferred Lies: a form of play sometimes permitted by local rules that allows you to move the ball within one club length in the fairway, usually because of adverse conditions (see **Winter Rules**).

Provisional Ball: a second shot hit from the same spot as the first ball, after announcing your belief that the first ball may be lost or out-of-bounds. If your first ball is in fact lost or out-of-bounds, your provisional ball is in play with two penalty strokes (stroke and distance). If your first ball is not lost or out of bounds, the provisional ball is picked up. The main purpose for hitting a provisional ball is to avoid having to return to the tee if the ball is not found or is out-of-bounds (the use of the provisional ball hastens the speed of play).

Pull: a straight shot that flies to the left of your target (for right-handed golfers). Opposite of a **Push.**

Punch Shot: shot used to keep the ball low, characterized by playing the ball back in your stance with a short backswing and follow through; useful for hitting out from under tree branches or on an especially windy day.

Push: a straight shot that flies to the right of your target (for right-handed golfers).

Read the Green: studying the green from different angles to determine its slope and the line your putt must travel to reach the hole.

Ready Golf: an accepted alternative to the normal order of play in which players who are ready to hit their golf ball do so rather than wait for players whose balls are farther from the hole, so long as they do not endanger any other player. The goal of "ready-golf" is to speed up the pace of play.

Release: the point during the downswing when the wrists uncock.

Royal and Ancient Golf Club (St. Andrews, Scotland): the governing body that determines the rules of the game for most of the world except the United States, which is governed by the United States Golf Association.

Rough: long grass bordering the fairway.

Sand Trap: another term for bunker.

Sandy: a term for getting up (onto the green) and down (into the hole) in two shots after being in a bunker.

Scramble: to recover from one or more poor shots; or a popular format for team play in which each member of the team tees off, the best shot is chosen, all players hit their second shot from that spot, and play continues in this manner until the ball is in the hole.

Scratch Player: a golfer who usually scores around par, someone with a 0 handicap.

Setup: preparing to hit the ball; including grip, stance, posture, ball position, and alignment to target (see **Address**).

Shank: errant shot caused by striking the ball with the hosel of the club. Such shots either dribble or shoot off to the right (for right-handed players).

Short Game: shots played from close to the green; including pitching, chipping, bunker play, and putting.

Sink: make a putt.

Skins: betting game for individual players or teams in which the lowest score on a hole wins the pot. If there is a tie, the pot carries over to the next hole.

Skull (Blade, Thin): to strike the ball at or above its center. Usually causes the ball to travel too far or not far enough.

Sleeve: box of three golf balls.

Slice: a shot that curves sharply from left to right (for a right-handed golfer); the most common error made by beginning golfers.

Slope: numerical value assigned to a golf course indicating its difficulty for average golfers, the higher the number, the more difficult the course. The average is 113.

Sole: the bottom of the clubhead; touching the ground with the bottom of the clubhead.

Stance: the position of your feet at address.

Starter: course official responsible for managing the order of play at the first tee.

Stroke: any forward movement of the club made with the intention to strike the ball.

Stroke (Medal) Play: form of competition in which the total number of strokes taken over one round, or several rounds, determines the winner.

Swing Plane: path the club travels around the body during the swing.

Takeaway: beginning of the backswing.

Tee: wooden or plastic support stick on which the ball is placed for the first shot on each hole, or the area from which the shot is hit.

Teeing Ground: area defined by tee markers at the beginning of each hole within which you must tee your ball. Your tee may not be placed in front of a line between the markers, nor more than two club lengths behind the markers.

Tee Time: your slot on the schedule of starting times, one every 9 or 10 minutes on a busy day. It's like a dinner reservation, except that it won't be held for you if you are late.

Tempo: the rhythm of your swing.

Through the Green: the entire golf course, excluding the teeing ground, hazards, and (putting) green.

Tight Lie: the ball is sitting on bare ground or very short grass, with little room for your club to get under the ball.

Touch: a player's ability to sense how far the ball will travel around the green.

Turn: go from the front nine to the back nine (from the 9th to the 10th hole); also the rotation of your shoulders and upper body during the swing.

USGA: United States Golf Association, the body that determines the rules of golf in the United States.

Waggle: back and forth movement of the clubhead in preparation for the swing. Its purpose is to help relax the player and promote a smooth takeaway.

Water Hazard: a permanent body of water (pond, lake, stream or drainage ditch) deliberately incorporated into the golf course design to provide a challenge to golfers. Removing your ball from a water hazard (or replacing one lost in water) incurs a one stroke penalty.

Wedge: a highly lofted club (iron) used for shots in which you want to maximize the time the ball spends in the air and minimize the distance it rolls after it lands.

Whiff: a swing and a miss. It still counts as a stroke.

Winter Rules: modification of rules to permit preferred lies in your own fairway (typically within one club length and no closer to the hole). The rationale for winter rules is to avoid penalizing players for imperfect course conditions (such as might prevail during the dormant season for grass or lack of course maintenance).

Index

About the Authors

David A. Goslin, Ph.D., a sociologist and former president and CEO of the American Institutes for Research in Washington, DC, has spent a great deal of time learning to play golf since retiring in 2001. He is the author or editor of five books including *Engaging Minds: Motivation and Learning in American Schools (2003).*

LPGA Master Teaching Professional **Mary Beth McGirr** was selected by *Golf for Women Magazine* as one of the "Top 50" teachers in the nation. She was LPGA National Coach of the Year in 1995 and the 2001 LPGA Southeast Section Teacher-of-the-Year. She is a guest instructor at Pine Needles for Peggy Kirk Bell's Golfaris, and at various golf schools around the country.